the
colour
design file

the colour
design file

Leslie Geddes-Brown

RYLAND
PETERS
& SMALL
LONDON NEW YORK

Designer Luana Gobbo
Senior Editor Clare Double
Picture Researcher Emily Westlake
Production Deborah Wehner
Art Director Gabriella Le Grazie
Publishing Director Alison Starling

First published in the United Kingdom in 2002
This revised edition published in 2009 by
Ryland Peters & Small
20–21 Jockey's Fields
London WC1R 4BW

ISBN 978 1 84597 826 6

A CIP record for this book is available
from the British Library.

Printed in China

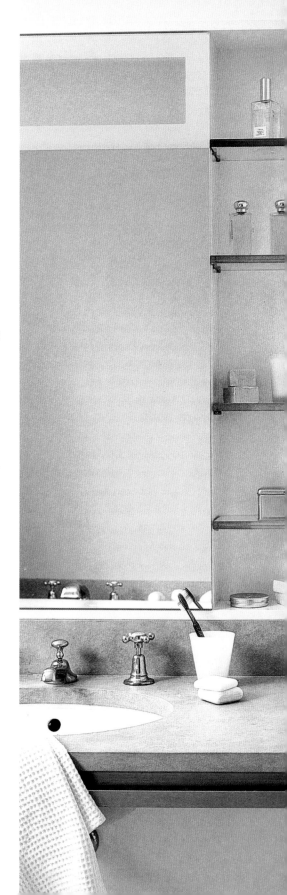

Introduction

This is a working book. Get it dog-eared and friendly, take inspiration from the rooms that are illustrated and then go and find some more. Stuff its pockets with your discoveries and use its blank pages for quick sketches. All the best designers, from Cartier to Loewy, carried notebooks constantly and it was from the ideas jotted down in them that their famous designs were created. One sketch is worth a thousand forgotten mental notes.

colour properties

To study colour and how it works, you need a new, technical, language. You're entering an area reserved for scientists and artists, whose job it is to learn how colours are made up and what they do.

With colour, you cannot believe what your eyes tell you; nor can you believe what you know to be true. Your eyes are affected by strong or feeble light; shadows are not grey, they are full of colour. Optical tricks will convince you that one square is larger than another when two colours are put together when, in fact, they are the same. Another trick is to look fixedly at a red dot for some time; transfer your gaze to a sheet of white paper, and that dot looks green. The dot which appears will always be the exact opposite of the original: red is transformed to green, yellow into blue. The reason for this is that your eye needs a change and only the opposite will do.

You, too, should be aware of the needs of your eyes. Too strong or too much of a colour will do you no favours, particularly if you want a relaxing

Above right **Reds advanc** to the eye to make a ro seem cosier. This living room uses two shades c red in a series of varyin stripes, which emphasi height while diminishin the impact of the red.

Above left **Oriental room** often involve a complex series of colours but it i the reds which stand ou

Below left **Warm and welcoming, yellow is th** lightest primary and lea likely to cause problem

atmosphere, and this is why skilled colourists will use a splash of a complementary colour to relieve a one-colour scheme. A vase of orange tulips in a blue room brings life and relief; add a large green hanging to a red room for the same effect.

Another problem in dealing with colours is that even the purest of them does not carry the same weight (tone is the official word). Some, like yellow, are always light; the darkest is violet. If you photographed yellow and violet together with black-and-white film, there would be plenty of contrast. Alternatively, if you were to team green and red in their most intense forms, you would find the black-and-white print came out grey, for both colours have the same weight.

Though the two can be used together, the amounts should be strictly controlled because, where colours of equal tone are teamed, the eye gets confused and unhappy. The answer, therefore, is to dull one or other colour so it is less intense.

The technical term for dulling a colour by the addition of black or white (white makes a colour more pastel while black introduces an element of grey) is to knock it back. And, when colours are opposites of each other, they are known as complementaries – confusing when the word generally means having something in common.

Above **With a neutral background, the softest colours can be highlights. Here the strongest ticking stripe emerges in charge.**

Below left **Apricot walls are set against pale cream and white. It succeeds because of the black touches.**

Below right **This room mixes red, yellow and blue successfully, but so pale and knocked back it works.**

Above left **A New York room, painted an 18th-century 'heritage' colour – a perfect background to the period furniture.**

Above right **A white lamp and woodwork give space to blues and tiny red notes.**

Below **This unusual room has wide vertical stripes of white, grey and pink on the walls. The eye can't quite sort out what's what.**

Despite working with them, I still find these technical terms confusing. The whole jargon of hues, tones, tints and shades is complicated because, in ordinary language as defined in the dictionary, many of these words are simply alternatives for the word 'colour'. However, it becomes important to use them correctly when dealing with colour suppliers or decorators because they will be using the technical jargon, so I've tried to explain these technical terms along with the working of the colour wheel (see pages 18–19). The answer is to keep referring back to those pages to make sure you always use the right term and eventually it will, I hope, become second nature.

How colours appear depends on the light. In the tropics, the hottest shocking pinks and vermilions are at home, while cool blues just vanish.

The next complication about how we see colour is that it changes with the light. In daylight, details are brought out sharply because the shadows become darker and the lit areas brighter. Thus, in a plain white room, the area hit by daylight will seem several shades lighter than the wall which has the window (and therefore the least light). Artificial light varies depending on the source. Neon is harsh and bluish, ordinary tungsten bulbs much warmer and friendlier. Candles even more so: recently an 18th-century ballroom was returned to its authentic colours of orange and green and no one could understand the choice – until the room was lit by candles.

In a yellowish artificial light, yellows become washed out – it's as though you were looking through a yellow filter. So reds become more orange, white turns creamier and purple goes brown. Clever lighting will take advantage of these characteristics with spots, uplighters and downlighters, and bulbs which are differently coloured.

As always when experimenting with colour, it's sensible to experiment with its effects before spending money on an expensive new scheme.

Above left **White as a secondary colour in a room strengthens whatever other colours are used. The apple green of this simple bathroom gives a pleasant cool minimalism where the only decorations are piles of towels and a quirky lamp.**

Above right **Pale green, which can be a seriously cold colour, is here transformed into an exciting ice-cream room by mixing it with casual touches of brilliant purple and pink. The greys of the bedhead and throw give added warmth.**

how we perceive colours

The perception of colour is extremely personal. I know –
where I see blue, my husband sees green. So when you
use colour, it's important to trust your own judgement.

Men tend to suffer more from colour blindness than women. At its rare
worst, this blindness turns every colour into grey and it can be spotted by
those cards which make up numbers in two colours of identical tone. Colour-
sensitive people spot the number at once; the colour-blind cannot see it at
all. Most of us, however, may see colours differently with different eyes. My
left eye, for instance, makes a scene more greeny; my right makes it pinker.

For many reasons, lots of us do not appreciate the real value of colour.
This is partly because we are not trained to look at what we actually see.
The Impressionists revealed as late as the 19th century that clouds were not

Opposite left **Earthy reds
and yellows colour this
apartment. The bedroom
has been panelled with
paints and washes, their
colours picked up in the
cushions and bed throw.**

Below left **Red is the
strongest colour and one
which advances towards
the eye. It is difficult to
use, but good in less lived
in period rooms.**

Above **An already warm
yellow and orange room
gains more of a glow by a
combination of mellow
lamps and the fire's
flames. The pattern of the
beams is emphasized by
the many sources of light.**

Below **Black is the colour for night-time rooms and, with its matt walls, the perfect background to avoid distraction in a billiard room. The distressed white columns add a neat touch of classical drama.**

Bottom **A large, airy kitchen appears even larger and friendlier with the choice of cool blues and whites. In the whole room there is nothing but a variety of these colours, plus the wood of counters and furniture. It's very seaside.**

grey and black but violet, puce and orange, and that the brightness and shadows cast by sun through a window were lime green and turquoise.

Looking at the works of the great painters is an excellent start in training our eyes really to see colour. Look at the works of any Impressionist; at Seurat and the pointillists who created scenes by painting multiple colours in dots, the Blaue Reiter school of painters in Germany or the Fauves in France. All took colour to its extremes.

We can use their skills to create interior schemes: watch how some colours – notably blue – recede to make a space apparently larger, while others – red is the obvious one – crowd in on the eye to reduce the same area. A point of red in a blue room will jump forward; a wall of bluey green in a yellow space will give the effect of distance. Similarly, we see some colours as warming and others as cool. But how we use them depends on the quality of the light as much as the central heating.

the colour wheel

Look at the colour wheel to learn what professionals mean when they talk about complementary colours, harmonious colours, hues, tones, shades and tints. What these terms mean is not obvious.

Below left You can get away with the most daring colours if you treat them with care. This city kitchen is in true shocking pink and floored in blue (with a pinkish tinge). It works because the band of stainless steel acts as a neutralizer, as does the detail of a white skirting between pink and blue.

Below right The strength of the lime green walls in this eating area is made visually possible by using its complementary strong red for the chair fabric. The absolute contrast between the two colours allows the eye to relax. Note, too, how the green is reflected in the tabletop.

For example, using the English language correctly, you would imagine that a complementary colour was one which complemented or went with another. Technically, however, a complementary colour is one which is the exact opposite on the colour wheel. Red therefore complements green, yellow is teamed with violet, crimson matches lime green. These colours fight with each other – but a little aggression in a room scheme is not a bad thing.

Colours which are harmonies are the exact opposite of complementaries in that they adjoin on the colour wheel; violet, bluey purple and blue or green, lime green and yellow. Colour harmonies which span only secondary and tertiary shades are easier on the eye than ones which take in a primary, such as red, crimson and violet.

The descriptions of hue, intensity and tone are all technical terms for the character of a colour. Hue describes the actual colour, its quality of blueness or yellowness. You might describe a colour as lemon yellow or greeny blue, for instance. Intensity (the word 'saturation' is also used) quantifies the purity of the hue, its brightness and density. At maximum intensity, it is strong and clean with nothing added to reduce the colour. When a colour is dimmed or muted by the addition of a duller hue, it is 'knocked back' or 'dirtied'. Don't imagine, however, that a knocked-back hue is by definition worse than a pure one – it is just more subtle.

See the box opposite for a description of more colour terms.

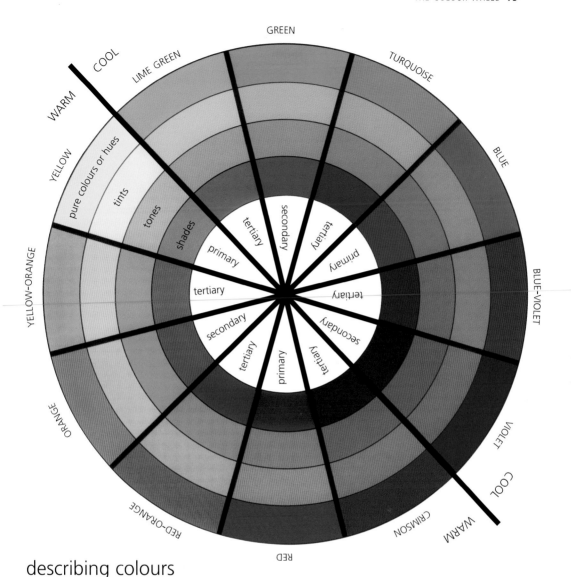

describing colours

The system of identifying colours and using them to best advantage revolves around the colour wheel, above, which shows how one colour bleeds into another and why.

In the wheel are the three primary colours – yellow, red and blue – along with three secondary colours, each of which is made from a combination of two primaries. These are

violet, orange and green. Finally there are six tertiary colours, which combine a primary colour and the secondary colour next to it. These are turquoise (blue and green), lime green (green and yellow), crimson (violet and red) plus three nameless colours created from the combination of orange and red, yellow and orange, and violet and blue. These hues appear

on the outside of the wheel above. Note that the wheel excludes neutrals – cream, beige, brown – and black and white.

If you add a darkening agent to a primary colour, you create a shade. So crimson mixed with burnt umber will be called a shade of crimson. The 'shades' ring above shows the pure hues plus black. If you mix the crimson

with white, it technically becomes a tint. The second ring above shows tints. Tone is how dark or light a colour is. The third ring shows tones (colours plus grey). Imagine a black-and-white photo. If everything in it were the same grey (the same tone), then the whole picture would be a single, blank colour. (The more tone produced by the photographer, the more contrast on the print.)

using complementary colours

One of the hardest decorative challenges is to mix these colours. These are the strongest, gutsiest schemes, which demand skill in balancing and placing different hues.

A complementary colour is the exact opposite of another on the colour wheel. Red versus green, yellow versus violet. If the two are used in their most saturated form, then it's hard to avoid a clash. Worse, some complementary colours are of equal tone, like red and green. In their pure form, if these two are put together in large amounts, you'll have a very unhappy room.

Complementaries can, however, work. Only use them when you want a strong-boned, lively effect – these are not combinations for cosiness. Thus they are good for rooms where relaxation is not a requisite – halls and landings, entrances, some formal dining rooms and busy kitchens.

Below **Complementary colours of tomato soup and grass green (with citrus yellow chairs added to the mix) were inspired by a 1968 kitchen designed by modernist architect Richard Rogers. Areas of black and lack of pattern are the key to why it works here.**

Above left **A strong and stylish kitchen is achieved by using complementary colours of bright yellow and a softer ultramarine blue. A single piece of furniture, simply painted, works the miracle.**

Above right **Even the smallest and most informal of spaces can be coloured to suit an overall scheme. The plainest white crockery separates the complementary colours of blue and yellow.**

Right **Kitchens are ideal areas for a bit of adventurous colouring, because they are meant to be lively rather than relaxing. Complementary orange and blue are slightly softened by the centrally placed tiles.**

Far right **Not, perhaps, a room to linger in, but this combination of brilliant orange with two blues makes an exciting way in.**

To create a room with complementary colours, make sure you first paint large areas in your chosen hues because these, above all, can affect each other. Next, ensure that, of the two complementaries you pick, one is knocked back or lightened so the overall tone is varied. When one colour is right, experiment by knocking back the second until both are comfortable together. Of our examples here, one uses an almost pure orange but teams it with a muted blue; another combines two muted shades of red and green with a twist of purer green for the chairs. Both are stylish and determined schemes from which smaller details and colours have been ruthlessly removed.

colour and light

Create serenity by avoiding contrasts. Soft and subtle changes of cool colour in uncluttered spaces induce a feeling of calm, light and pleasure, while deep colours can add drama to darker rooms.

Colours are usually more loaded with symbolism than we appreciate when picking them from the shade card. The positive primary colours are all about action. The reverse is the case with the whiter shades of pale. The minute gradations by which white turns to cream or grey can all be used to evoke a sense of tranquil calm. These are the colours to use in spaces for relaxation.

Don't, however, equate calm with boredom. These serene shades take considerable skill to manage and you will also need to be extremely disciplined in choosing how to furnish them. Unplanned clutter must be avoided – though, as you see from the photographs, planned pictures or objects can still be soothing – and so must outbursts of dramatic colour.

Right **The strong light and architectural detailing of this apartment means that the room can be treated with maximum simplicity.**

Below **A series of light sources around this hall allows a scheme of soft blues, greens and greys to come alive. A motley collection of chairs has been painted in similar shades and even the watercolours and sketches are chosen to fit.**

Left **A strong light filtering from an unseen source above the stairs gives a fine welcome to this English entrance hall in a country house (also shown above). This means that the decoration can survive being muted. A painted floor increases the lightness.**

Below **Sheer white fabric at the window diffuses the light to create a cool, dim effect which is increased by the shadowed white of the room. Chairs and walls are in similar shades.**

Bottom **Rooms with big, beautiful windows, especially those above ground level, get stupendous light. Take advantage of the subtle effect of similar colours.**

You can plan everything in a room or a corridor around the most meticulous series of colours and objects and then wreck the entire effect with a single jarring note. Imagine, for instance, a red throw tossed over the banisters of the light-filled hallway opposite. The area would be entirely different. The same goes for a friend in a scarlet coat, but even the most controlled designer has to allow for friends in the wrong clothes.

When you are dealing with these serene shades, it's clever to vary the palette inch by inch. The ceiling can be a whisker paler than the walls to give an impression of height; the detailing of cornices or window surrounds can be subtly enhanced by using several different shades of the same colour to deepen carving or mouldings. Floors should be worked into the overall effect: pale floors which lead naturally to the colours of the walls increase space and reduce change. They always lighten a room where it is most needed.

Furniture, too, can be painted in with your scheme to add tranquillity. A tint lighter than the wall will bring it forward and emphasize its shape; a shade darker will make it recede.

Obviously, the colours you pick for a room are directly concerned with the quantity and quality

Above **Mirrors and their lookalikes (here the bright steel of the washbasin) can increase the amount of light in a dark room.**

Above right **A landing and glimpsed bathroom are painted in a series of deep, warm yellows in an area which relies on light from below.**

of the light available. Does the room face north? This is the light traditionally picked by artists because it throws no strong beams or shadows – the light is more overall because sun doesn't shine in a north-facing room. Such rooms for non-artists need to be given excitement through colour rather than light. I would avoid grey, for example, though white and cream will both add light. But jazz them up with touches of scarlet for warmth. I would, however, avoid too much yellow because it is such a cliché in dark or unsunny areas.

Dark rooms can also be made more interesting by opting for a dark colour – especially if these are basically night-time rooms. Spare bedrooms and dining rooms come to mind – I have a semi-basement spare bedroom papered in dark green stripes. It's dramatic and cosy.

Rooms which have the benefit of strong sun are much easier. They can be as neutral as you please, for the sun will provide the light and drama, or they will take easily to strong primaries. Think of the sun-drenched paintings of Matisse, all primary colours, or street scenes in tropical India.

Don't stick with a single tone when you are painting chairs and tables – even matched sets can be tweaked into soft contrasts.

Below **Apart from the glowing abstract painting, this modern take on a Georgian room is painted in colours so subtle as to be virtually indescribable. Soft taupe is teamed with coral and the window surround washed with a tint of blue. The generous window gives enough light to play on these neutrals.**

Smaller areas of sunlight – in small-windowed cottages, for instance – need to be treasured. Make sure no curtain cuts out the light when drawn back, and paint the window surrounds a lighter colour to get the maximum from it. If you can, enclose the view outside by making sunny small windows like pictures with ornamental frames. In such rooms, paint walls which get any sunlight a lighter, brighter colour, or hang them with mirrors to double the quantity of the light. The saying 'It's all done with mirrors' is particularly apposite when working with colour and light.

Above right **More generous windows allow this busy room to breathe. The colours are all versions of heather – at least six – used with verve and skill. Pattern, however, is limited to the bold checked chair.**

Right **Light, and the impression of a garden beyond, flood into this bedroom painted with all the texture and variation of a single apricot. Voile curtains emphasize the feeling of light.**

Opposite below **This highly feminine scheme of pink every which way must have these large, light-filled windows to survive.**

zoning and defining space

Using colour, you can quickly hide ugly features and emphasize good ones by creating different zones in different tones. It is the easiest and cheapest way to make a building do what you want.

Open-plan living was one of the innovations of the 20th century and it continues as we colonize old factories and warehouses left empty by the second industrial revolution. These buildings offer huge spaces, high ceilings and factory fittings which need their own special colour treatment.

With the disappearance of formal rooms designed for a single purpose has come a way of defining a particular area within a larger space for a special purpose. This is done by lowering a ceiling, creating an arched niche, unfurling a screen or subtly changing the colour scheme and lighting.

An area for eating, for instance, will benefit from a lowered ceiling, dimmed or hanging lights and darker colours; kitchen spaces need good,

Above **A huge space joined by wide arches has been zoned by using charcoal in one area and pale taupe beyond. But the overall parquet floor provides continuity. Though the zones are distinct, the same black, grey, white and tan mix throughout.**

strong lights around worktops and light, indeterminate colours which let the food and equipment speak for themselves. Living areas should offer relaxation and this means space, light and comfort. Other parts of an open-plan apartment need to tell you what they are: corridors should be sectioned off from the main rooms by a change in colour and lighting, while private areas should subtly tell visitors that these are no-go areas.

Curiously, these complexities seem to work better with schemes which are not too subtle. Perhaps it's because industrial buildings were never designed

Above left and right **Architects like monochromes because they sharpen a room's details. Here Voon Wong uses a palette of greys, the darkest of which defines the open-plan (but lower height) eating area.**

Right **This Glasgow room shows the difference between ordinary and inspired use of colour. The broad horizontal bands are painted in deep earth tones, culminating in black and topped by a surprising band of burnt orange – and various paint effects are also used, from matt to gloss to metallic. The low tables with bright vases complete the whole.**

to be sophisticated in the first place. Strong variations teamed with plenty of white really sing in an open-plan area and, if you are trying to zone parts of it, it will be have to be done with conviction. No one will spot a new zone if it is just painted in a beige one shade darker than the rest.

So work with primary and complementary colours, carefully schemed. In an overall white space, a single red wall will offer not only a warm welcome but also attract the eye (and encourage you to move towards it). At the end of a corridor, a sheet of scarlet will beckon. A strong yellow primary on a far wall suggests a source of hidden sunlight while soft or dark blue speaks of privacy. Don't, however, let colours become clichéd: crimson is not ideal for a dining area; malachite green or indigo is comforting by artificial light.

In a large open space, you may get natural light from unexpected quarters. If so, make the best use of the surprise by using colours which stand out in natural light. White and variations of blue-white and pale blue all look stark and abstract used opposite windows; dark colours like black, magenta and violet change hardly at all in strong sun, while primary and secondary colours are intensified and made glowing.

Above **Extraordinary stripes don't upset this traditional room. The rose, yellow and white ignore its structure.**

Below left **The large areas of white in this bedroom mean that the strong orange wall** only increases the space and coolness.

Below right **A loft uses strong yellows and scarlet to bring the walls forward, while the green behind the pillars gently recedes.**

Left **A strong lime in this New York kitchen is combined with softer colours which take some of the acidity away. These include a soft green, steel and blond wood.**

Below **Blackboard paint is fairly new to the retail market and can be inspiringly used, especially in areas like this dark hallway. An artist in the family can make regular changes to the sketch at the end. The light is an added visual treat.**

Dark colours used on lowered ceilings make the space seem smaller and more intimate, therefore good for entertaining, as do zoned areas in a large room painted in strong or dark hues.

Combining natural light with pale colours will automatically zone parts of an open space (you'll need to work out how to vary this after dark). You can increase the effect by varying very slightly the shades and tints on these areas. If the natural light throws one wall into prominence, making angles more evident, then let the lightest wall be in the palest shade, with adjoining walls and ceilings varied to increase the angularity. If natural light hits a white beamed ceiling, subtly colour the shadowed areas with a darker shade.

Coloured floors can also be used to zone parts of a space. A square of seagrass flung under a dining table will delineate the 'dining area' from the sanded boards of the living space; boards painted black in a niche will also describe a zone used for a new purpose. Kitchens should certainly be given soft, comfortable and contrasting matting which is easy to clean, is acoustically dulling and generous to dropped pots. It will also tell visitors that this is the cook's private space, to be entered only with an invitation.

colour highlights

There are two distinct ways of using colour in an interior. The first is in the broad basis of the design. The second is using colour as an exciting accessory.

Using accessories, as one does with clothes, should be witty, fun and unexpected. Unexpected because it's so easy. You can change an entire look by moving a few ornaments or cushions. You can change it for different seasons when winter's heavy curtains in deep red give way to spring's embroidered cotton in lime green, or the dark brown fur throw on the bed is replaced with a brilliant blue cotton quilt. You can change the style of a room as easily by removing the sienna tan French provincial pots and putting Chinese black lacquer in their place or by changing a brilliant abstract on the wall for an Indonesian batik in indigo. You can create effects almost by

Above **Glass is a natural attention seeker because of its shine and shape. To this add the brilliant colour of this display.**

Below **Two sets of unlined sheer curtains in different colours are a key factor in this large living room. The central obelisk, with similar-coloured ornaments, draws the room together.**

Left **This creamy living room, its architectural features painted in with the walls, relies for colour on the two orange throws and the cushions on the sofa. By changing the colour, the entire room would be altered. This is a summery scheme. In winter, the colours should be more sombre.**

accident, as I found when I put a pair of bright coral Chinese hat-stands (tall vase-like affairs) on a chest in front of a portrait. They immediately drew attention to the red sealing-wax seal on a letter clutched in the man's hand.

In fact, I think quite a lot of colour highlighting is instinctive. If you are like me, you will move objects about until they look 'right'. The 'rightness' is your eye appreciating the combination of colours and shapes you have unwittingly created. Without conscious thought, you will reject a mixture of blues which vary between the red and green ends of the spectrum or a selection of off-whites which change from creams to greys. Trust your instincts first, then work out why something looks right or wrong. Once you understand the trick, use it again.

Highlighting with colour also means using complementary hues to draw the eye where you want it to go. If you have a particularly fine view from a window, use curtains as you would use a picture frame: the

Above left **A warm yellow glaze has been brushed all over this Italian kitchen in a way reminiscent of a Pompeian mural. Below, the skirtings are treated in a darker terracotta.**

Above right **Clear straw walls (actually Hay by Farrow & Ball) bring together this enormous open-plan living space which combines cooking, eating and relaxing. The room also benefits from the quantity of different pale blues on doors, furniture and tablecloths.**

The skill with highlights is to know when to stop. The whole effect should look wonderfully casual and instinctive.

Top left and right **Strong light streams into these sugar-almond working areas (proving, by the way, that offices don't have to be dull). Large windows and natural daylight tend to bleach the hues.**

Above **An unseen light source strengthens and brightens the modern colours used in this bedroom-corner study and puts interesting shadows on the walls.**

curtains can be a brilliant attention-grabbing scarlet or, more subtly, a dark grey or black which highlights the colours of the scene beyond.

If you want to send out signals that a room is intended for relaxing, a combination of colour and texture will do the work for you: bright oranges, rusts and red, along with deep browns, will seem welcoming where blue and magenta do not. Fur and fleece and all manner of snuggly fabrics will emphasize the message. Thus chairs and sofas piled with soft throws and brilliant silk cushions in warm colours will immediately encourage people to lounge, and the use of these bright colours will make the easy chairs the focal point of the room.

In contrast, using a succession of cool tints will suggest calm and order, the highlight of the room being little more than a colour slightly warmer or brighter. In a scheme of light blue and grey, a tiny touch of pale coral will do the trick without being garish. Similarly, in a monochrome grey and white space, a single black object will assume enormous importance: it could be a basalt vase or simply a black-framed photograph.

Where subtle highlights suit subtle rooms, garish combinations are ideal for certain modern interiors. Think of the primary squares of Mondrian's paintings, Rietvelt's painted wooden chairs or Damien Hirst's coloured circles, and you will see how it can be done. The trick, once again, is to study the bright colours of your intended highlights. A phalanx of curvy Venetian glass vases should be controlled into one or two colours only for maximum impact; a collection of kitchenware in primary colours which have been slightly knocked back with white will breathe the freshness and bucolic good looks of a dairy.

I'm always harking back to fashion, and accessories in rooms should follow the rules of accessories in clothes: don't be too clever or too obvious; don't match too much.

Above **A Manhattan apartment has opted for a dramatic 20th-century look which combines pure white and black with the shine of steel and, everywhere, classic designs in an unabashed crimson.**

Below **Why not let crockery and equipment cheer your kitchen? The owners of these have bought mugs to match their units (left) and a range of rainbow bowls (right), displayed with artful casualness.**

finding your colours

When you decorate, first, of course, decide what your room is for and how you want the room to feel. Then consider how to add your own personal style. This is done by identifying great colours.

Faced with a blank room – newly plastered walls, wooden floorboards, no furniture – how do you go about transforming it into a decorative scheme? It's important to get the room's use and zones clear right at the start because the way you use colour thereafter will depend on that. And, in making the fundamental decisions, you will begin to have an idea of what style and colour you want to impose. You will begin to envisage that the living room would look friendly in a soft blue (not least because your sofa is covered in a good-looking navy – and you can't afford to recover it). But what blue? What colour of curtains would work and what floor?

My own response is to work with what I already have, because rooms where everything has been bought from scratch for a scheme look like hotels and because I am Scottish enough not to waste money. So, I'll probably start with that navy sofa and find a swatch of the fabric to pin on a board. Next, I'll look in one of those exhaustive paint swatches put out by

Above left and right **When you are working with complex colours, create your own colour wheel with artists' pastels, noting the name of each as you put it in position. Doing this will make you appreciate how colours change minutely as the spectrum alters. Another idea is to paint small boxes in the colours you intend to use on the walls. This will give you an idea about how each intensifies in an enclosed space.**

the mega paint firms which have thousands of colours with improbable names until I find a paler blue of exactly the same hue as the navy sofa. With luck I can then get a sample pot and paint a largish square on my board. Does it look right or should it be darker? Is it a pleasant colour for the room or am I being too clever with my matching? I'll keep the board beside me and think about it until I am convinced I'm right. If I'm not convinced, I'll try different colours: a bluey grey, perhaps, or would stark white be more startling?

With the main colour choice made, the next decision is how to work with it: do you want the room to use strong, complementary colours – scarlet with your navy, like a military

Above left Dyed shades of indigo have been put together in a colour chart which was not only used throughout a Swedish-style house, but has become part of the decoration.

Above centre Colour boards are always advisable – but don't have to be utilitarian. Here, flowers and scraps are temporarily framed.

Above right **This sunny blue bedroom recalls the maritime past of an American lighthouse keeper's restored cottage.**

Right **At least four greens and blues appear here. Touches of white and tan create a casual zone.**

Far right **Matt mint green paint creates highlights and moody shadows.**

Below **A range of golds, tans and browns has been used by designer Geraldine Prieur to create a very French living room with classically stencilled walls.**

uniform – or ones which harmonize, like turquoise or pale grey? Again, personally, I start looking at lots of other interiors in books and magazines to get some inspiration.

Once I've found a basis for what to do next, I start adding to my swatch board: a scrap of fabric, perhaps, or a postcard of a lively painting (the Italian Renaissance painters had a particularly good line in brilliant pinks working with sky and lapis blues). Otherwise, I might look at combinations which work in the garden – delphinium blues with *Alchemilla mollis*'s lime green, dark green ceanothus leaves and strong cobalt flowers with white Shasta daisies – or which can be found in nature. Walks on the beach to find mussel shells (near-black blue with shiny mother-of-pearl) or sea-washed glass can bring ideas to the surface, as do trips to galleries and museums. Walk in a spring woodland and you will find the combination of a carpet of bluebells under the unfurling misty lime green of the beech leaves to be magical.

If you have your paint colour chart with you (I know it's a bore), try to pin down exactly the colour of the bluebells

Right **Indigo and dark purple are the base for a bright, near-clashing, array of rose, scarlet, yellow and shocking pink.**

Don't let a decorator hurry your decision. If you get the colour wrong, you must start again – good news for him but not you.

and exactly the shade of the beech leaves – not as individuals, but en masse. Colour is notoriously tricky to memorize.

Luckily, not every colour scheme depends on long country walks. A bowl of fruit, apples, apricots and raspberries can start you thinking. Buy what you can and start to arrange them (redcurrant may be just what you need with that navy). Look for combinations which work in the greengrocer's or food market. Stop at florists' stalls, buy what you fancy and add a vaseful in front of your swatch. Clothes, too, are an inspiration, especially the work of top designers. Scrutinize shop windows for clever mixtures of colour and pattern in clothes and how they have been positioned by the dresser.

Lastly, never be too proud to copy, whether it's Botticelli, a beach or Balenciaga. Artists and designers make no bones about looking everywhere for inspiration and nor should we.

Above left and right **Monochromes can be some of the most exciting and dramatic colours to use in generous rooms. Here, the architect Voon Wong plays with a whole manner of textures and patterns but, ever so occasionally, he bursts into colour. The thin red metal line behind the eating area is inspired, as is the touch of blue among the cushions.**

Opposite below right **Playing with whites creates cool and subtle rooms.**

soft furnishings

One of the most important considerations in using colour is texture, because it can materially alter how the colour is perceived. Fabrics, therefore, have to be chosen with skill.

Below **Bright grass green appears on the cupboard-door curtains, on the chairs and on the wallpaper with its fabric design. A generous old quilt covers the table and imparts texture to a countrified dining room.**

Soft furnishings are the ultimate accessory because what you do with them will dictate the style of a room. Though your colour scheme may call for upholstery and curtains of, let's say, a brilliant lime green, the effect will be entirely different if you choose velvet or tweed. The velvet subconsciously speaks of luxury, formality and urbanity, while in tweed the room will be aligned with the countryside (even of a sophisticated, Chanel-type country in lime green), with warmth, winter and a certain casualness. So it matters.

What also matters is the ability of the textile to take a dye. Silk is famous for the way its colours glow as though backlit, and it is also able to define

Above and opposite below **A range of soft indigo-dyed fabrics are teamed with painted furniture in this Swedish-style house. A clever touch is to use blue-and-white gingham in two different-sized checks. The colour chart is on page 35.**

minute variations of colour. Many manmade fibres seem to have the opposite ability: take a fine colour and dye Crimplene or Polyester in it and the result seems tawdry, slithery and unpleasantly shiny. It's also sadly the case that the best results are invariably achieved with the most expensive materials.

Wool can take dye well and, when woven as tweed, minute variations can be added to the yarn so that what, from a distance, may seem a warm conker brown becomes at close quarters a complex mixture of primary colours. At the far end of this scale are the traditional tweeds of Harris and Donegal, where large chunks of brilliantly coloured wool are added to the yarn mix and then woven in at random by hand.

However excellent in the deep dark shades, wool will never produce a pure white, the best being a pleasant fleecy cream. Nor does silk, possibly because its texture adds slubs and shadows. For pure white, the answer is the cool fabrics of cotton and linen, which have traditionally been used for bedding, canvas and blinds. Cotton also takes well to quilting, appliqué and lace, where pattern can be added without colour.

Above left **Plain ticking is a contrast to more colourful Chinese wallpaper.**

Above right **Simple ticking stripes on the bed contrast with the complex green stencilled walls.**

Above **White is never just one colour. Here, blue-white walls look greener with off-white plaster cast, photo mounts and floor.**

Below **Play with white rooms by accessorizing them: here the hanging, books and even the watch strap add plenty of pink.**

Linen, now a luxury fabric, has more presence than cotton and can be found in chunky weaves akin to hessian – all those bleached linen sheets, for example, which are now fashionable as neutral curtains. It can also be woven to a fine, silky finish or, combined with cotton, made into a strong, friendly fabric ideal for loose covers.

Both cotton and linen take dyes extremely well. Linen has been used in Europe since medieval times as the basis for multi-coloured patterned fabrics, while Indian-influenced chintzes arrived in Europe in time for Samuel Pepys to marvel at them in his diary. ('Chintz' means 'multi-coloured'.)

When you are planning how to pick from such a huge variety of fabrics, yarns, colours, weaves

Cotton is rarely woven in complex patterns and is easy to wash and iron. It's perfect for pure white fabrics in constant use.

Below Large bathrooms can be treated like any other main room: great quantities of transparent cotton in bleached colours make this one a haven.

Bottom Bedrooms generally have a large amount of white linen and, in towns, lend themselves to monochrome schemes.

and patterns, it's good to be disciplined. Silk can work with tweed but it needs careful handling; linen and cotton are fine together but their colours and weaves need to be controlled. You can stick to, say, blue and white and mix the patterns and weaves or, alternatively, you can mix the colours but control the pattern: a series of *toile de Jouy* scenes in their typical rose madder, tobacco and indigo shades will work well together. I also find it's good to control the period. Many 18th-century fabrics will mix well – the toile with a typical large check, for instance, or those minute multi-coloured lining fabrics which back single-shade curtains with charm and interest. The 1920s enjoyment of strong reds and oranges means they look good with such accessories as Clarice Cliff's Bizarre pottery, while Pre-Raphaelite heavy crimsons and gold look well beside William Morris's sumptuous patterns.

Left An eerie death mask, bandaged chair and knotted nets are cheered up no end by the heavily textured and brilliant acid yellow cord curtains. The texture of the parquet is thus emphasized.

Below The secret of using brilliant white – and making it look whiter than white – is to team it with off-whites. This bedroom adds stripes of dull beige from floor to ceiling.

paint finishes

We're lucky today to be able to buy so many different paints: matt oils, wood stains, transparent varnishes and old-fashioned milk paints, from around the world.

Where, thirty years ago, the amateur decorator was limited to the bland productions of the major firms, where oil paints were always gloss and strongly coloured and emulsions always satin and pastel, today we can produce any effect that we want. As always, of course, multiplicity of choice doesn't make life easier. If you are skilled at painting and decorating, it will make the end result better; if not, then not.

Paint finishes are also ruled by fashion. Today gloss paint is out. We've suddenly discovered that there's actually no need for our skirting boards, windowsills and panelled doors to shine as though constantly sprayed with water. They can be matt or, better still, have their colour enhanced where

Below left and right **It's always a good idea to throw out preconceived notions about using paint. These two rooms use colours in bold vertical stripes, but the stripes' colours are not repeated. The room on the right also varies the paint finish, from matt to metallic.**

Left **Such bold simplicity could only be Colonial American. Clear red is used on dados and around the window, with yellow in second place. Blue chairs add the third primary.**

Below **If orange paint has brown added, it becomes an earth shade and will work in warm climates. This bedroom, however, combines the orange with neutral browns, to cool it.**

necessary by the application of one of the many furniture and metal waxes which have also come onto the retail market.

We've also discovered that skirtings and doors don't, by God-given regulation, have to be paler than the surrounding walls. They can be darker, which makes sense anyway since scuffs show less. Thanks particularly to the National Trust and Farrow & Ball's work with authentic paint colours, we've also found that off-white doesn't have to be magnolia, a colour I hope is consigned to outer darkness for a century or more.

A fascination with authenticity has also led to the reintroduction of all those 18th-century techniques of dragging, ragging, rolling and scumbling (softening a colour by rubbing or

Below left **Unpainted plaster has a beautiful pink finish which can be copied in paint (so it doesn't rub), as in this distressed background to an Art Nouveau scheme. The choice of browns and golds brings out the brown of the pink background.**

Below right **A detailed close-up shows how the warm plaster effect is created with washes of paint and varnish. The muted creams, browns and pinks should be brushed on in many layers.**

You can paint virtually everything in a room – walls, doors, floors, furniture, lamps – to achieve perfection. One artist painted his pet birds, too, but this is not recommended.

Top and above **An Italian apartment uses Renaissance paint colours such as sienna, terracotta and saffron to create brushed abstract murals** on the walls. **The effect is similar to the distressed murals discovered at Pompeii, though they, of course, had added figures over the washes.**

applying paint with a dry brush), which we first used as they had been 200 years ago but which are now being updated. The transparent varnishes and opaque finishes which came on the general market, along with the implements and skills involved, are now being put to different uses. It is possible, for example, to alternate matt and shiny finishes in large, hand-painted stripes either vertically or horizontally; or different random patterns such as dragging and ragging can be used geometrically on a single wall. As always, such fanciness needs severe control or you will feel you are inside a kaleidoscope but, carefully sited, a single worked-over wall can be as effective as a large abstract painting. Indeed, it really is a mural.

Papers which have recently come onto the market have included quantities of metallics. Don't be put off by their constant appearance in expensive hotel bathrooms – they can actually look stunning. The metals are not just silver and gold, but softer aluminium and copper and menacing bronze or zinc. Such papers should, again, be used with restraint. Think of them in the same way as a gilded picture frame or mirror, and they will glitz up a dull room satisfactorily.

We've also lightened up a bit in our choice of paint colours and where we use them. Doors are no longer painted a single colour which ignores their panels – different areas are now coloured separately, either in complementary hues such as blue and yellow, in strong contrasts like black, grey and white or, more casually and easily, in shades and tints of a single colour.

Paints specially formulated for floors have also appeared on the market. These are a real

Right and far right
Decorative paint techniques have never gone away since their revival in the 1980s, though care is needed to avoid the excesses of that decade. Here a warm orange and red palette is created by washing the walls a pale pink then ragging a darker shade on top. Extra interest comes from doing this in stripes. The doors are painted to resemble watered silk.

help if you want to keep the plain boards (or can't afford a carpet) but the actual wood doesn't stand up to scrutiny. No amount of sanding will hide inferior soft wood, but a stain or opaque layer of paint will. If a room is dark, liming or painting the floor a shade of white will brighten it up no end, while a dull area can be enlivened by a painted pattern on the floor to imitate a geometric carpet. Waxing these boards improves both the paint's longevity and its appearance.

Below left and right **The ultimate in wall finishes is found in this Milanese dining room. The walls, apart from a dark blue arch, have all been covered with genuine gold leaf.**

• Explore a garden in winter to appreciate neutral values, from the silvery heads of pampas grass to bleached reed leaves and the soft browns of fir cones.

• Seed-heads appear in all the neutrals: shining honesty circles, waxy cream lupin pods, blue-grey poppy-heads and lacy dandelion clocks.

• Beaches have inspirational features such as chunks of white-covered flint, morsels of broken limpet shells and sea-bleached glass.

• Neutrals often appear when objects have died or been bleached by wind and sun, as in old flower-heads and old wooden buildings.

• Baskets of stripped willow, chestnut shavings or plaited rushes are all complex mixes of bleached or grained neutrals.

• Most paper is neutral in tone, but note the wide variety in texture, from chunky handmade to the warmth of cheap paper bags.

• Old fabrics take on a neutral appearance with age, with backgrounds that look tea-stained. Use real tea to dull and distress reproduction cloth or prints.

• Neutrals are used in nature as camouflage. A careful study of tortoiseshell, deerskin, brown trout scales, thrush eggs and owls' feathers will demonstrate their subtlety.

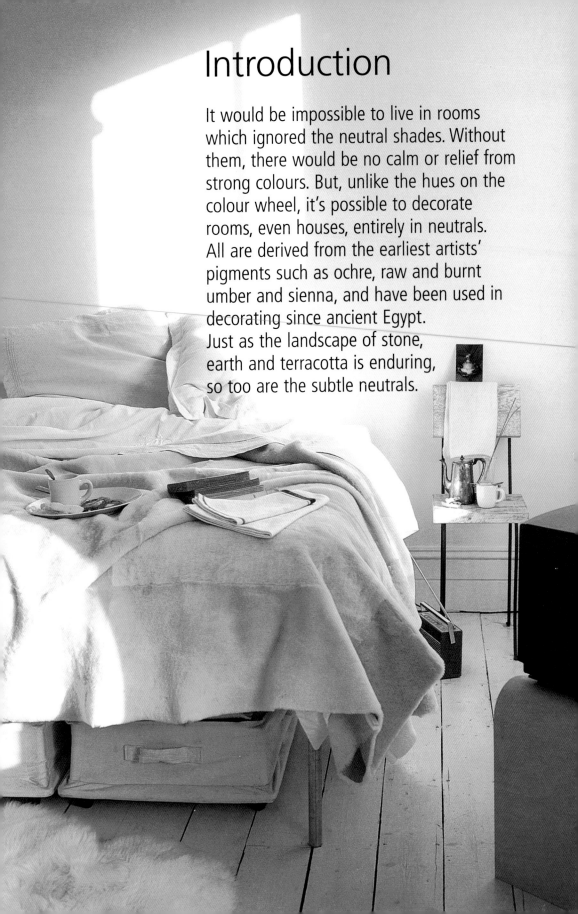

Introduction

It would be impossible to live in rooms which ignored the neutral shades. Without them, there would be no calm or relief from strong colours. But, unlike the hues on the colour wheel, it's possible to decorate rooms, even houses, entirely in neutrals. All are derived from the earliest artists' pigments such as ochre, raw and burnt umber and sienna, and have been used in decorating since ancient Egypt. Just as the landscape of stone, earth and terracotta is enduring, so too are the subtle neutrals.

whites

Working with a pure white palette is unforgiving but always rewarding. Its textures and tones evoke a calm and freshness which are at home in city or country.

Until you start to plan an all-white room or area, you may not realize that white comes in as many different shades, tones and tints as does blue or green. There are whites which are greenish in colour, those which are backed with blue, black or yellow. Then, because white picks up and reflects the light, it can vary by texture. Think of a white silk velvet contrasted with a white tweed. The shadows of the hairy tweed will give a totally different overall effect to that of the smooth velvet.

Below **White is the best colour to use if you are undecided how to cope with a space. This large ex-industrial area has been given a white once-over – brilliant on the walls and slightly scuffed on the floor, with inexpensive covers on all the chairs.**

It is hard, but rewarding, to work with white alone. Hard, because it's important to consider every single element in the space. You will need to get swatches of all the fabrics, samples of every paint and, before that, have your daylight and artificial lighting worked out. It is equally important to consider whether you want gloss, eggshell or flat paint, and where. It's also essential, because this is the most unforgiving of colours, to consider how you will live in an all-white room and, if the answer is frequently, then decide how you will keep it clean. Dirty all-white rooms are extremely unpleasant.

One way to bypass some of these decisions is to divide white into two categories: one set of whites which are based on blues and blacks, from bright white to various shades of grey, and another set made up from browns and yellows – the beiges and creams. It is a good idea to work with only one set. Currently, the greys are more fashionable, but the creams are always warmer.

Ever since I've been decorating houses, I have opted to have every room painted in various shades of white while I make up my mind what

Above left **Virtually everything in this apartment living room is pure white or neutral, which makes the unruly hydrangea in a sexy lilac shade stand out. The effect is transient, too.**

Above right **This all-white scheme is given drama by the strong black-and-white abstract and relief by the** bookshelves. White cotton covers on the chairs can be washed frequently and kept pristine.

Below **Pieces by top designers – here Marco Zanuso's armchair and the 1927 plastic chair by Heinz Rasch – are given centre stage in an all-white scheme. The op-art French standard lamp is 1960s.**

In a white room, everything fits in with everything else: when you rearrange or want to buy more, there are few complications.

This page **The owners of this Malibu barn have used nothing but white (apart from the black Chinese cupboard), to draw attention to the complex roof beams. White and antique wood are natural partners – especially in the case of the reclaimed cupboard doors (top right) which are dry-brushed and distressed. Even the floors are whitened to show off the structure.**

final scheme will work best – it's the equivalent of giving your sofa a loose cover in unbleached calico. This is because pure white will let you evaluate the feeling of a room, its angles and areas, its moods and movement, until you can come to a firmer decision. Meanwhile, plain white will be comfortable to live with and easy with whatever furniture and colours you are considering. And, of course, if the entire house is painted in this single neutral, then you will be able to move things around, decide the uses for rooms and whether there should be specific zones for working or eating.

No other colour will have this effect. I would go mad if my entire house was painted magnolia or yellow and, while I could live happily with a soft blue or grey scheme, I don't think that the blank canvas of the rooms would

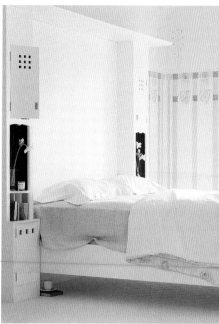

be quite so blank. White, while it makes plenty of statements, is comfortable and adaptable.

One of my firm beliefs is that all household linen is best left white, so you already start off with plain white sheets, duvets, towels and flannels, napkins and bathmats. If you have got used to the same plan, you will know how incredibly easy it is to wash them and still find them looking pristine each week.

I also live in several rooms which have white-painted floors, and everyone loves the effect. The rooms are cleaner, brighter and lighter, somehow more friendly and approachable. Yes, the paint does wear off to look like wood with a limed effect but that doesn't matter in the least. Other friends are more particular, painting and washing their all-white stairs and floors so they are always immaculate. This attention to detail gives a strong air of luxury while being miles cheaper than any form of carpet (though not, of course, particularly saving in time).

The same goes for white curtains and upholstery. Though it shows dirt immediately, white fabric is no worse in this respect than black or scarlet: any pure colour will mark easily. Where white benefits, however, is that it will wash perfectly because the only pure whites available in fabric come in cotton and linen (we'll ignore all those manmade horrors, which do wash

Top left **Even a converted warehouse can be made romantic by using white antique textiles. Lace, muslin and a gauzy dress, the apparent antithesis of loft living, are restrained enough to succeed.**

Top right **Charles Rennie Mackintosh's Hill House inspired this delightfully serene bedroom in an Arts and Crafts house in Wales.**

Above **All the whites combine in this beautifully calm bedroom, which seems entirely transient. Pride of place is given to the perfect bed linen.**

There is no better setting for food than a white background. Add exhilaration to a white kitchen with piles of tomatoes or lemons, boxes of earthy potatoes and ropes of creamy garlic bulbs.

but look and feel horrible). Wool and silk can never bleach to the pure, blue-white of cotton. As a result, it's possible to fill a room with beautifully laundered white fabrics which are slightly scented with fresh air and cleanliness, while (where necessary) being knife-pleated in folds after recent ironing.

In kitchens take the same line – there's lots of plain white crockery available, most of it the cheapest on the market, while plain transparent glasses are honorary whites. Look at minimalist John Pawson's views on kitchens to see how white on white will work in even the busiest cooking area. White crockery, transparent glass, brushed steel and plain marble tops are allied with neutral floorboards and quantities of cupboards to hide the frankly gaudy boxes of cornflakes and tins of baked beans.

Above **Allow the colours of fresh produce to sing by creating a silver and white kitchen: floor painted, tiled, and starring an old fridge.**

Below **When a room is all white, the only two objects in other colours take pride of place. The quirky topiary is one – but see the toast.**

Right In a minimal-style kitchen, all is white and steel. Even the floor and glass-fronted cabinets are carefully colourless.

Far right White is the colour of minimalism. Two whites – creamish and bluish – are contrasted here.

Below Virtually everything here is wood, black or white. The boards are varied to suggest zones.

WHITE IN COMBINATION White is so clean and pure that it is the perfect antidote to strong colour: flags have white backgrounds against which brilliant primaries are shown at their best.

National symbols are often on white because they will show up against a clear blue sky or a dirty red-brick block, and they will cope with attacks from other strong primaries – the red, white and blue of France against a yellow facade is lovely; the red and white of Japan on an ultramarine sky is thrilling; and the yellow and blue of Sweden against a red-painted farm is moving.

Above **This French holiday house gets brilliant light and reflections from the North Sea. The owners have used the same sea blue to create a stylish but comfortable living room.**

But white can cope with subtler combinations too: look at it on these pages with soft grey-blue fabrics or stronger indigo blues. Consider it with a pattern of lime green leaves for a conservatory or garden room, with red in a gingham-covered country kitchen or alongside Chinese red lacquer or the pink in a *toile de Jouy*. It's fine with every kind of brown, from stone to country tan to the deep umber of ebony furniture.

Teamed with very strong and dark colours, white is dramatic. With its opposite, black, it takes on a starkness beloved of architects and photographers. Teamed with scarlet, cobalt and green, it adds a freshness which the colours alone do not automatically possess, while with neutrals it provides a contrast which emphasizes the very slight element of colour in their shades. Off-white becomes even more off-white; cream becomes creamier, and the blue shades of grey more evident.

It's a colour which is equally at ease in town and country, in grandiose rooms and quirky cottages. To emphasize detail, use slight variations of grey or cream to pull out the highlights.

Below **The banisters are painted just a shade bluer than the quilt seen below them. A rural scheme.**

Bottom **The strong blues of these curtains and cushions recall the sea view from the French windows on sunny days.**

creams

Cream has been having rather a bad press recently, but once a colour has been unfashionable it can then be rediscovered. I believe this will happen with cream.

The colour cream is exactly what it describes – double cream, whipped cream, clotted cream. It's a colour that is warm, friendly and rich. In too-large quantities it can also be indigestible and sickly. It is also somewhat bland, so if you are brave enough to opt for a cream scheme (brave only in that it's unchic – it's perfectly easy to work with), you should pick your room carefully.

In my view, cream is at its best when used with strong-boned architecture. Even more than white, it is a nothing colour which disappears, a soft background on which other elements stand out. Thus, if you are lucky enough to have huge

Above **Blond wood with pale cream is always soothing and stylish. This dining room benefits from the pattern introduced by the cane-backed chairs and toile cushion, but everything else – even the tabletop – is painted as bland a cream as possible.**

Right **In this English house, built in 1906, the owner has used a simple palette of creams, browns and mingled neutrals to let the Arts and Crafts architecture take first place.**

windows, a wonderful view or columns and cornices, then cream can work well. The larger and lighter the room, the darker the cream can be.

Cream is excellent for panelling, especially if you use several shades together. To make the most of light in the room, paint the largest flat areas in the lightest tone, using darker shades for the mouldings and surrounds. If the room is very light and needs more warmth, then the reverse is true.

It looks good, too, in small, rural rooms, whether living areas or bedrooms in tiny cottages. In this case, the tone should be of a single cream, a warm white which will hide the lumps and bumps on an old wall or make the most of the light emerging from little windows.

Above left **An apartment in Milan is worked in overall cream to create a haven from the heat and bustle outside. Cream, because it is a warmed white, is good in both summer and winter. Here, again, the cream is allied to a series of tans and brown, from picture mounts to parquet.**

Above right **An overall creamy effect in a room can be created by using simple fabrics in the shades of off-white that both linen and wool naturally fall into. By using a bland cream background, this room relies on textures for its interest: the lines of rug and chair plus the grid of the old chest alongside.**

Left **This large apartment space has been effectively de-zoned. A series of creams, backed up by several shades of tan, from carpet to furniture, ensures that this spacious area is considered a single unit. It is serene, relaxed and entirely formal.**

In Hollywood the epitome of luxury was cream carpets, wall-to-wall mirrors and ice-cream-coloured satin sheets. A similar effect can be seen in the Art Deco rooms of some grand London hotels.

Thus, if you have a good-looking room with something special about it, do consider cream in all its tints and shades. Curiously, despite its blandness, all-cream rooms are extremely stylish. Go for broke with an all-over scheme which includes curtains, carpets and soft furnishings while making sure that, for instance, what wood is visible is dark and exotic. Ebony would be fine, as would rosewood.

Change the textures in the room while keeping them the same colour. Use tweed with satin, suede with chrome, slub with appliqué, embroidery and quilting. Get the lighting exactly right with table and wall lights and hidden spots in the ceiling, for cream works best with an overall glow heightened with stronger beams to show up interesting areas.

Above **If they are kept in the same series of shades and tones, creams and whites evoke luxury, simplicity and warmth. This utterly plain bedroom manages to do all three by limiting pattern and ornament to a minimum.**

Right **This townhouse bedroom uses a flat matt paint to cover the charmingly naive Georgian panelling and plain bed. Plain floorboards, a cream Roman blind and some darker sprigged fabric for bed linen completes the scheme.**

Above **Bathrooms respond well to cream because the colour is both neutral and warm. If, like me, you always have white towels, they look good too.**

Right **Cream tiled walls, lights and floor, along with soft white bathroom fittings, are allied with wooden furniture to create a stylish pre-World War II bathroom which is both comforting and luxurious.**

Above **The Hollywood bathroom par excellence relies on the strong grid created by overall cream tiles and the white fur rug over the cream floor. But everything is subordinated to the period double washbasin.**

Have plenty of pictures, too, on those bland walls. Nothing too bright or violently coloured, but sketches, prints and watercolours mounted in sepia and gilt, bright white and birds'-eye maple. Abstracts in shades of brown, black and cream look wonderful.

To be really old-fashioned in the most stylish way, make your kitchens and bathrooms cream schemes. Huge square baths and washbasins should be surrounded by cream tiles and lots of built-in mirrors. Piles of fluffy white towels and a soft cream marble floor are the stuff of Hollywood too. Kitchens, on the other hand, should be given an old-fashioned cream Aga (solid fuel, of course) with lots of those curvy kitchen cupboards and fridges so popular in the 1950s. Actually, it's a colour which really works with food and is also very calming for the cook.

CREAM IN COMBINATION Despite its neutral character, cream is a surprisingly difficult colour to combine with others. It's averse to too many varied colours or clutter, too much prettiness or drama.

Above left **A mix of creams and near-browns has been used for a modern version of a Georgian living room. Note how the chimney breast starts forward because it's so much lighter – and how the grey striped sofa stands out.**

Above right **Taking the Ben Nicholson abstract above the fire as its inspiration, this room combines all the creams and tans within it (including the black fire surround) then departs from its severe squares into sensual curves.**

Right **Cream teamed with other allied neutrals. The scheme works because of the top-quality furniture: two Jacobsen Egg chairs alongside a curvaceous sofa and table by Kagan.**

Perhaps the best way to start off using cream with other colours is to think of it as an off-white. Like all such hues, cream responds well to a monochrome treatment – black and cream is highly sophisticated, as are the deep browns of ebony and mahogany. But only one at a time.

It also looks splendid combined with another single light tint: a soft pink, coral, sky blue or even grey, each of them dulled down with the addition of white or black to the original colour. The second colour should not be obtrusive but simply add richness and a focal point to the room. Again, it's best to be strictly disciplined and use only one single colour with the cream.

White is probably the easiest of all because you don't have to choose it carefully to fit in with the red or yellow base of the cream. From soft muslin curtains to firmly woven rugs or ironed bed linen, it can hardly be beaten.

Here a thoroughly neutral background of matt cream walls is used to point up some very eccentric French furniture. A wobbly mirror by Osvaldo Borsani is echoed by wobbly gilded wall lights at each side and René Drouet's curvy-legged glass table. The old gold armchairs are by Leleu.

beiges and browns

Beige and its darker sister, brown, have less pink in them than cream and are therefore considered more 'masculine'. Ridiculous, but you know what I mean.

Now, happily, there's no more nonsense about men's dens and women's boudoirs, and brown is at last being used as it should be. It's a colour as strong and powerful as black, though rather more friendly. It is also one of the most natural of colours – like green – seen all over the landscape.

We are, thus, very at ease with brown, which is considered warm and relaxing. Brown and beige are the colours of every wood, from the darkness of ebony, red of mahogany, tan of oak to beige of beech and birch. The more tropical the wood, the darker and firmer it gets.

So brown and beige are excellent backing colours – waxed oak and elm floorboards, limed old panelling and log-cabin ceilings. Objects placed against brown or hung on beige walls respond with glowing gilt frames or silhouettes firmly outlined. As in nature, it's almost impossible for different kinds of timber to look unhappy together. Think of marquetry and parquet floors and make the most of it.

Browns and beiges are natural in fabrics, too. Unbleached linen is a soft beige, wild silk comes in a charming range of pale tans, while natural wool from rare-breed sheep emerges looking just like the animals. Think, too, of the camouflage colours of zebras and giraffes, leopards and tigers – there are excellent manmade copies available.

The beige-brown range can be exciting, exotic, comforting, warm and intimate as well as strong, minimalist and mannered. It's up to you.

Opposite page top and centre **Browns rarely clash with each other, so mix them at will. The items on this bedside table pick up the room's donkey brown, white and cobalt.**

Opposite page bottom **Brown, white and cream is a gentler mix than black and white. Chocolate walls and floor team with ebony and a beautiful old quilt.**

Above **Slubbed, textured silk in warm nut browns hangs horizontally in this bathroom. With white and cream added, the room is warm and enfolding.**

Below left and right **This bathroom mixes browns from palest beige walls to parquet floor and darker brown bath. A mirror, and towel rail with dark brown towels, add decoration.**

BEIGE AND BROWN IN COMBINATION Despite its strength and presence, dark brown is still a neutral hue, while beige is the neutral par excellence. Both are extremely forgiving to work with.

Unlike cream, whose pinkish base can cause problems, beiges and browns are rarely unhappy with other colours (except, of course, cream and different versions of brown or yellow). These are ancient colours based on earth tones and thus soft on the eye and, literally, part of the landscape.

Beige and brown are fine backgrounds for really strong, stinging colours – shocking pink, lime green, brilliant blue, especially if the strong colour is used with discretion and in small quantities. But they are also excellent with each other, or with other near-neutrals like Swedish blue or pale olive green.

Really smart schemes today also put brown and beige with black and white to create designs which are exceptionally strong because they are

Below **Arts and Crafts houses generally have an affinity with cream and brown schemes because the style made full use of the colours of timber. Here the various ways of working with wood and its colours are given full play.**

virtually monochrome. The stark black and white give the brown or beige an extra edge, making it become almost a colour.

Browns and beiges are also useful in period schemes. If you are furnishing with antiques, the chances are that these will be of brown wood – teak, birch, satinwood and fruitwood. Grander pieces may also have painting, ormolu and gilding. Presumably you will want the furniture to take pride of place, and the way to do this is to give them a neutral but similar background. Both dark brown and beige will do here, depending on what overall effect you want.

In general, 18th-century furniture will look better with a lighter background, for its lines are fine and subtle, while later furniture, especially stout Victorian pieces, can easily cope with dark brown. Another fashionable period is Arts and Crafts furniture, with its strong, vernacular lines in more rural timbers. The characterful woods of oak, elm, sycamore and cherry look especially good in brown schemes; the solidity suits them.

Top **This house exploits the full brown range. Mellow wooden furniture and windows join drab upholstery and cupboard.**

Above **A room celebrating the natural browns of wood and leather. The panelling is stained to add to the depth of colour.**

greys and silvers

My own preference is for this range of neutrals. I could live in a house which uses nothing but white and black with the greys ranged between them.

Behind the suspended white wall of this uncompromising living room are a series of greys, from the pale walls to the mixed greys of the sofas and their cushions. The room is rescued from coldness by the warm African hardwood floor and welcoming fire.

I could also live with no gold, using nothing but silver, steel and aluminium for picture frames, kitchen worktops, bathroom fittings and door handles. Indeed, my living room has silver and cut glass knobs and fingerplates, rescued from an old hotel.

Greys, of course, come in all kinds of mixes – pink-greys, yellow-greys, blue-greys and brown-greys – and, as usual with colours, it's best not to mix them together. My own preference is for the blue-greys, though I do appreciate that these can be cold. Yet, with central heating available, I don't think the idea of warmth is important in urban areas. I like the space and sophistication that silver and grey offer town houses, especially

Top **This room's palette is all greys (even in the artwork) and a neutral dark brown. The whole is made possible by the dark-painted brown floor.**

Above **A monochrome scheme is rescued from coldness by purple chairs.**

those with period features like marble fireplaces (often grey themselves), cornices to offer a variation in detailing, and ornamental doors. Subtle changes in the shade of grey can be used to highlight fine features.

Grey and steel are almost essential in modern and minimalist homes, from all-aluminium kitchens whose only decoration is shelves of glasses to bedrooms made comfortable by using textured grey flannels, cashmere and faux fur.

Rural houses perhaps should be decorated with slightly warmer greys – the colours which hover between beige, bone and string. These greys are more allied to earth tones, variations on burnt umber and sienna, which chime particularly well with the landscape outside.

The final advantage of these colours is that they are extremely easy to live with. If I were starting out with a new house, uncertain about decor, I would paint the rooms in greys and live with that until I'd formed more long-term ideas. I'd do a room at a time, leaving the surroundings grey until I had decided on something different.

Top **A conversion decorated in a series of off-white and greys. The blond wood floor is the perfect foil for the lighter colours.**

Above **Bathrooms' natural tendency to silver and grey is exploited here with** a translucent glass sheet and steel basins and tops.

Left **This stylish bathroom was simple to achieve: everything is grey, white or silver. The mosaic tiles and rough gown contrast with the polish of the steel tub.**

blacks

You have to be brave to use black as the major part of a scheme, for it has scary connotations: of night, death and the devil, of claustrophobia and caves.

I have seen all-black rooms – one bedroom complete with black ostrich feathers on a four-poster and with skulls as a bit of light relief – and have never felt I wanted to linger in them. Black as a background unrelieved by other colours seems to suck much of the life out of a room and either to deaden or overemphasize whatever other colours are used.

Personally, therefore, I would not consider a room of unrelieved black. What I would do, however, is use black on a single wall and combine it with lighter tones of grey or soft, charming colours like pale coral, sky blue or –

Below left It may look all black but this room corner exploits black's variations, from blue-black walls to the browny black of the fireplace. The early-20th-century metal screen adds needed texture.

Below right Blackboard paint in a dark corridor. The white Jack light is poised in it like sculpture.

Left **A Manhattan apartment uses black with white and tan to stylish and simple effect. The matt black wall is relieved by the textured Japanese pillows and the woven seat of the 'Greek' stool. The black-and-white photograph is pure drama.**

Below left and centre **Two views of an apartment in Antwerp show a bedroom where black has been used to enforce the modular effect of beams, cupboards and rug. Even the exotic flower photograph has been left unframed. Pure Mondrian.**

lovely, this – shades of violet. Black, too, works on a single wall which is covered with pictures or collected objects (not just black-and-white photographs, however, as the contrast is too strong).

Matt blackboard paint looks good on single walls which are then used for graffiti, notes or, for the confident, large sketches and diagrams. It's a nice idea because it is so versatile, and is especially good in children's rooms.

I just might use black in a corridor or on a dark landing where rooms open off with an explosion of colour, or in a show-off dining room used only at night and for entertaining. In fact, it is the epitome of a show-off scheme: people only use black when they want gasps of astonishment and the affectation of theatrical drama – which is why it's a nightclub colour.

Above **The rough and grainy texture of natural slate, used in giant slabs to tile this bathroom, means that the dense colour is somewhat broken up as the faults catch and reflect back the light. The two mirrors and lots of steel equipment also brighten a sombre room.**

This picture and below Introduce even a speck of colour into a monochrome palette and it bursts out of the background. The spiky green plant provides not only colour but an unruly shape, as do the scarlet anemones in a severe living room. Neither area would be as exciting without these touches.

GREY AND BLACK IN COMBINATION Both provide a marvellous backdrop for colours, and are just as good with other neutrals.

Because grey and black are pure and cool by nature, they make a perfect foil for the full-strength saturated primaries: brilliant scarlet, bright yellow or dreamy ultramarine. You can even use them with complementary colours, to provide clear, uncomplicated areas between the different hues.

If you look at art galleries, both national institutions and private galleries selling modern works (many extremely bright), you will find that most are decorated in grey, white and black, because these shades are so welcoming to colour.

Most contemporary houses are also given grey and black backgrounds and this, too, is because they suit the clean lines

and uncluttered spaces which are inherently modern 21st century in style.

Modern architects like these shades because they flatter a building's details. This means, equally, that 17th-, 18th- and 19th-century rooms can benefit from their attention, too.

Grey particularly is a superb foil for gilding – for examples, look at French chateaus' panelled rooms – because its coolness flatters the richness of gold. Its use makes walls seem to be larger and to recede, which is valuable if you are positioning single focal points of strong colour. This may be no more than a single jungle leaf in a vase or a curvy 20th-century scarlet chair. Against the grey, it will immediately attract attention.

Black and grey are also very good at defining an object's shape. Place a white marble sculpture against a black wall and its details are emphasized. Even more striking is the way pure black and grey backgrounds, by their strength and discipline, combine well with the odd undisciplined object – an indoor tree or vase of curving tulips.

Above left and right **If you use grey with white, it will sharpen both. This open-plan apartment combines a series of dark grey wall panels with brilliant matt white furniture and objects. It looks amazing, and is easy to achieve.**

Below **Another very simple scheme teams a series of monochromes – white, black, mottled grey suede – and furniture with strong hangings. But the painting and framed mirror add only blue, orange and yellow to the whole.**

COLOUR CONTROL

Whites, creams, beiges and browns
are invaluable, providing calm areas between bursts of lively colour. They are natural shades – seen in the landscape – and therefore an important part of the scenery. However, in using this palette, it's important to divide the pink- and yellow-based hues from those with green and blue in their makeup. Pink and yellow neutrals are the creams, mellow tans and conker browns, and they work fine together. They look very unhappy if you mingle them with cooler neutrals, off-whites such as string and bone, and soft grey-beiges based on chalk and stone. Keep warm and cool versions of these hues apart and your schemes will be happy.

Greys, silvers and blacks
While black is the drama queen of the neutrals, white is the coolest (as in hip) colour of them all. Between them comes a whole range of greys which are, despite the name, far from boring. Just as both black and white may have a background colour (try matching blacks and you will see they can verge to the blue or the red), so does grey. Currently fashionable is the blue and green range of greys. Don't mix them with pink and yellow greys. White also varies a lot, and you can use it to effect with several variations in a single room. Stick to, say, a blue-based series of blacks, greys and whites, and they will work extremely well together. All the range is extremely flattering to strong colours and can accept several complementary primaries at once if the balance is right.

- Always use test pots of neutrals to get the mix right but, unlike strong colours, smaller areas test-painted will be enough.

- Add swatches of fabric for upholstery, carpets and curtains to your test board because texture is very important in neutral colours.

- Neutrals can be mixed in quantity – you can get away with six variations in a single room – and don't need added strong colours.

- But strong colours live happily alongside neutrals, which provide space between each colour so they don't buzz and clash.

- Neutrals are good on painted furniture – either make pieces darker or lighter than the background. Colour a matching set in different shades or a harlequin set in the same shade.

- Use white for sunny walls, for ceilings that need height and for zoning welcoming areas.

- Black is hard to use in large quantities. Keep its drama to a single area, and counter it with grey and off-white rather than brilliant white.

- Grey not only works in several shades; its changes can give decorative emphasis to panelling, cornices and other architectural detail. The paler the grey, the more emphasis.

- Grey is the ideal background for metallic shades. Panelling can be gilded, silver frames will add glitter, while duller zinc, mercury and aluminium echo its colours.

- Grey can be combined with strong primaries but, in an all-grey room, a subtle touch of soft pink or blue will appear more strongly coloured.

- What seems to be a simple colour — yellow, red or green — is in fact a complex progression across the spectrum. You need to match colours carefully, for a greeny yellow may look dreadful with a reddy yellow.

- Affordable pink and purple dyes were only invented in the 19th century and were rarely seen before that. If your rooms are of an earlier date, it would be inauthentic (but not necessarily wrong) to use them.

- Subtle schemes can be invented on a colour board, such as that above. First assemble views and photographs which inspire you, such as the pebbles and seaside rooftops, then add swatches and paint colours which suit them.

- While neutrals can work without any strong colour in the scheme, strong colours nearly always need the addition of neutrals to look their best.

- Ask yourself if the beautiful vista you've snipped from a magazine will actually work in your room. Mother-of-pearl looks lovely in an oyster, less good in the office.

- Similarly, is it sensible to conjure up sea and sand in a 20th-floor apartment in a city centre? It may be, but think about it first.

- Don't be scared of bright pink or purple. We are put off by the mass of gloomy Victorian rooms which used these newly invented colours quite wrongly.

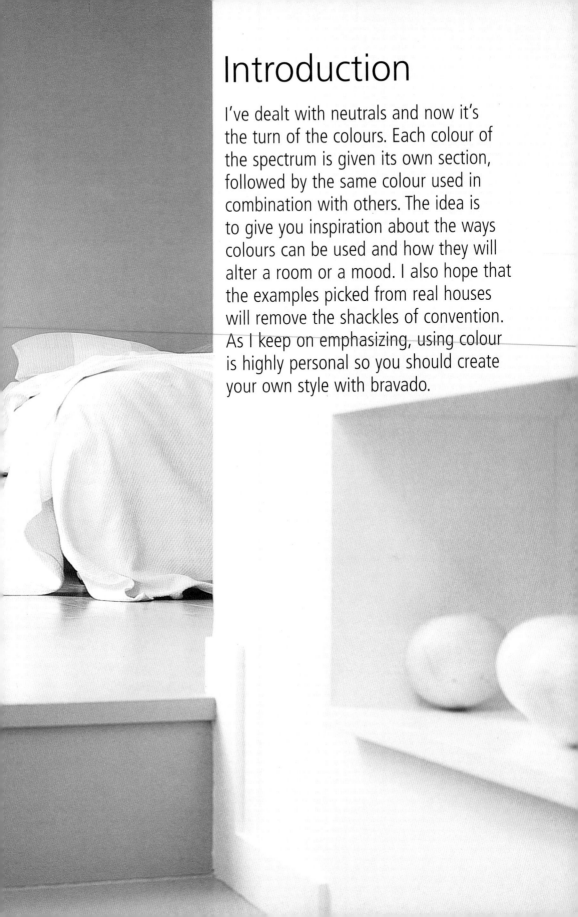

Introduction

I've dealt with neutrals and now it's the turn of the colours. Each colour of the spectrum is given its own section, followed by the same colour used in combination with others. The idea is to give you inspiration about the ways colours can be used and how they will alter a room or a mood. I also hope that the examples picked from real houses will remove the shackles of convention. As I keep on emphasizing, using colour is highly personal so you should create your own style with bravado.

blues

I know it's personal, but blue to me is one of the easiest and best colours to use. Because blue has so many shades and subtleties, it is infinitely adaptable.

'Infinitely' is a word I've chosen carefully because blue is the colour of infinity, the clear sky blue that is magically created through millions of miles of empty space. It is the colour of distance, faraway moody blue hills, lakes which are miles deep, the sea and misty mornings. So we value the colour that reminds us of the best the landscape can offer.

Blue is also a colour used in those pictures we love the best: the blue of a Tuscan sky behind the blue of the Virgin's robe in a Renaissance masterpiece, the Mediterranean dashes in a Matisse window-scape or a Dufy racing scene, the blue in Jasper John and Mark Rothko abstracts. And, of course,

Below **Here an outdoor room mingles blue-green cane furniture with floral fabric and pot plants – not forgetting the garden greens outside.**

Opposite below **The only pattern in this moody blue room is in the striped bed hanging, which emphasizes the simple lines of the white-painted bed.**

the blues found in all the best palaces from the stinging tropical tints of India to the mirrored pomp of Versailles.

To come down a peg or three, I have used blue wherever I have lived, from the dining room of my family home, painted a dark ultramarine, to my present dining room, papered in wide and deep blue stripes. The living room here in London is an indeterminate bluey green which is ideal for coping with pictures, books and objects while, in the country, the large and rustic kitchen copies that of the National Trust's Calke Abbey in being painted a strong but knocked-back ultramarine, the colour of those old blue bags you once put in the wash.

Blue, according to the historians, has the ability to deter flies, which is why it was traditionally used in kitchens, dairies and larders. It's difficult to quantify this, for who knows how many more flies there might be in a red kitchen?

What it does prove, however, is that blue is a truly adaptable colour. It can adorn the roof of a Gothic church, a Renaissance palace, a Victorian dairy or a Corbusier cube. At the ultramarine end of the range, it is warm and lively; at the Prussian and indigo end, it is cool and breezy.

While it's not a good idea to mix different ends of the blue spectrum, within each hue there is a huge variety of shades

Above left and right
Indigo-dyed fabric and the matching paints in various strengths are wonderful to work with because, from the deepest navy to the palest washed-out denim, all are in harmony. They also work in all kinds of rooms, from bedroom to garden room, and from country to town.

A tiny shower room in a London apartment has been recreated as a shipboard bathing area. Not only is the whole painted in shiny paint of a typical marine blue, but the window has been turned into a porthole. The stainless-steel fittings are reminiscent of a luxury yacht. This is an example of coping with a tiny space by emphasizing it.

Far left **Blue has an affinity with bathrooms like this, where mosaic tiles give a minute variation to overall colour. But see how cleverly the distressed brass and bronze of taps, radiator and pipe provide the second colour.**

Left **A whole busy wall of various blue mosaic tiles needs the calming influence of diffused light from the window, which is covered with translucent corrugated plastic.**

Above left **Blue walls and shadows cast by textured mat and tiles are cleverly united by using a dark navy on the base of the old iron bath.**

Above right **Using blue and white adventurously in a bedroom removes the colours from cliché. The six different shades and tones of blue are all variations of an airforce colour scheme. Note, too, how the textures vary.**

and tints. Blue, mixed with white, varies from the palest, near off-white to a stunning range of cerulean and French blues; combined with black it offers subtle blue-greys to the darkest midnights.

All these mixtures can be arranged together – think how indigo and denim work as clothes, from the palest washed look to dirty denim. You can use ethereal blue as a background and pose dark navy against it, or simply contrast the pale tint with a duller, knocked-back grey-blue.

Blue with blue in patterns is almost invariably successful. Think of stripes and checks, tickings and wax-resist batiks of indigo, or of the more complex toiles and single-colour floral chintzes. You may well use them as fabrics but you can also find them turning up as wallpapers and even carpets.

Use mixes of blue on furniture, too, especially in the country or if you are beside water. All blues obviously have an affinity with water, not only because it becomes blue but because navies, flags, fishermen and sailors all deck themselves in blue. So do policemen, but that's another story.

BLUE IN COMBINATION Many successful blue combinations have a maritime link. Draw on the many tones of the sea on a sunny day, and pair blue with green or yellow to create intimations of a beach.

Blue and white is so common in everything from crockery and Cornish ware to batik hangings and striped awnings that it is almost a cliché.

But blue is happy with almost any colour as long as their values are carefully controlled. For example, the complementary colour of scarlet provides a really exhilarating mixture, even though, if also combined with white, it is too reminiscent of a country's flag. But many flags are red, white and blue because the combination is so vibrant against a pale blue sky.

Chinese red lacquer – or walls of this peculiarly intense colour – looks wonderful with blue, either ultramarine or indigo. I know, because a pair of red lacquer leather trunks stand in my library against the palest green-blue wall. The red looks just as good with French navy or darker midnight.

It is just as forgiving of orange, one of the more frightening colours to work with. Blue with orange may not be restful, but it's lively. The same goes for shocking pink. You can even put the three together (see the pictures opposite).

Calmer mixes are blues with greys and blacks which, if the three colours are all of the same tone, make a near monochrome scheme ideal for modern rooms and large loft areas. Similarly, warmer blues sit well with browns and creams.

Of all childhood sayings, 'Blue and green should never be seen' is one of the silliest. Blue and green come from the same part of the spectrum and fit extremely well together. Of course, it's important to work with greeny blues and bluey greens rather than red-based blues and yellow-based greens, but your eye will tell you that.

Above **French limestone flags, gleaming steel and white are all used to strengthen the brilliant ultramarine of the handle-less kitchen cupboards.**

Top **This building was once a water reservoir, so the owner has chosen a watery blue for a mosaic tiled bathroom, overlit by a single, circular skylight.**

Above and right **Searingly hot areas of orange and shocking pink are balanced in this extraordinary apartment by even larger areas of dark navy and dark turquoise. The chairs are an even darker blue. This scheme is clearly inspired by the Mexican architect and colourist, Luis Barragán.**

Blue with green is very evocative. These colours are in the many tones of the sea on a sunny day, they come together where fields meet a sunny sky, they mingle in a peacock's tail. So use them to create this lyrical feeling of the country or beach. When you have found the perfect pair of blue and green, then pick which is to be dominant in your room. Blue, on the whole, is a colour which recedes, while green is slightly more forceful. Blue will add space, green will bring features nearer.

Generally, I would pick blue as the major colour here for that reason. But there's always a compromise in turquoise – a difficult colour, but a perfect partner for both. Touches of turquoise can therefore help bring the two together into a scheme based entirely on seascape shades.

When blue is teamed with yellow, the effect is likely to be warmer than with green. It is more important, however, to consider how each works on the other. Soft blue mixed with soft yellowy cream will produce a calm,

Below left Has the owner matched the cool tones of the kitchen to the collection of jugs, or vice versa? If you do have a collection on display, make the most of its colours in your decorative scheme.

Below right A strong country blue is used throughout this kitchen: not for just walls but detailing on the drawers, the pattern of the tiles and the pans. The white floor ties everything together.

Bottom right Two tones of indigo blue are teamed with two of grass green.

Blue and white is a widely used mix, but that doesn't mean you should ignore it. One decorator lived with nothing else.

romantic room, but otherwise it's not a good idea to use both colours in the same weight because both are strong primaries and will fight. Like green, yellow advances objects, but feels warmer.

The variations of both are just as important – blues can be green-based or red-based, while yellows vary from red-based egg to green-based lime. As a rule, keep to one or the other. Also, buy sample pots of the paints you intend to use and paint at least a square metre before deciding.

With a blue-yellow mix, keep other colours to a minimum. Whites, creams and blue-greys are the best companions because they are neutral.

Top **A French-inspired room mixes a grey-blue with the softest of yellows, backed by white and other neutrals. This is a relaxed room for a country house.**

Above **All distractions have been hidden away in this large kitchen to increase the sense of space. A series of blues is used for the same reason, since blue is a receding colour. The white floor and chairs add serenity and light.**

greens

Green is the strongest of the secondary colours and acts like a primary. Though it is a mix of yellow and blue, green has a clear character of its own.

Unlike, say, turquoise or purple, where both primaries are clearly evident, green's mixture of blue and yellow creates an entirely new hue – but one that is extremely well-known to us. Green is the predominant colour of plants. We pride ourselves on our smooth emerald lawns, our combination of green shades and shapes in topiary gardens and on the riot of tropical palms and banana trees in the holiday brochures.

Green, therefore, is a good colour to work with, because not only does it offer large variations of hue, shade and tint, but also because it is restful and pleasant without the reclusive quality of blue or the demanding presence of yellow. Curiously, too, both ends of the green spectrum can live happily

Below **Green is a very amenable shade, perhaps because we are so used to seeing it in nature mixed with strong, bright colours. This living room is given dark green multi-coloured marbled walls the colour of olive leaves, which are the perfect background for strong Eastern embroidery and Fauve paintings.**

together, which is not the case with most other colours. Turquoise, at the far blue end, and lime green at the yellow, can be teamed as long as one is firmly knocked back.

On the other hand, it's rather harder to combine various shades of green. While racing green, at the deep end, and emerald or malachite can be put together, a mixture of dark green and pale is instantly reminiscent of school corridors, hospital wards and other unfriendly institutions. Worse still is the same in gloss. Never use it.

Nor is green ideal for a bathroom, though it was much used there in the 1950s. This is because it is essentially a cold colour, inimical to stripping off on an icy morning. Or maybe that's just because I was brought up in an unheated house with a green bathroom.

As a result of this perceived coldness, I love green in hot rooms such as conservatories where, of course, it flatters the living plants.

Above left **Is it grey? Is it green? This indeterminate colour adds sophistication to this corner for gazing.**

Above right **The greyest possible version of green is rubbed and distressed** over a bedroom wall. The shade is picked up by the cushions on the red bed.

Below **The boldness of the woods is offset with leafy green walls and china. The picture combines both.**

Dark green is the colour of smart cars and Le Mans racers and, used diplomatically, will recall the ultra-chic 1920s and 1930s. In this case – and only in this – it can be used in gloss or lacquer.

I like it in dining rooms, either light or dark, where it avoids the pomposity of deep red. It's good in urban schemes, which need as much connection with nature as they can get, and it is excellent with complex detailing. Green looks best of all on panelling, even Rococo panelling, on classical cornices or with special features emphasized by a different shade or gilding.

In the 18th century, green was an extremely expensive colour to make up and, as a result, became highly fashionable. You will see the smartest pea green in many a picture of an authentic interior of an aristocratic town house, whether in London, Paris or New Orleans. Now that paint colours

Below **This interesting scheme is in the beige, brown and off-green range of colours. The chairs are original Ambrose Heal, as is the table, made for Winston Churchill. The designer has covered the tongue-and-groove panels of this room in an indeterminate shade of greeny brown to join the strong natural shades of the wood.**

are all the same price, you can get the look at an unfashionable fraction of the cost.

Dark green, especially a shade combined with plenty of black, seems to be just the right colour for earlier architecture, of the 15th and 16th centuries. This is partly because it's a sombre colour well suited to the heavy architecture, beamed ceilings and small windows of the period. It is an ideal background for a heavy tapestry or for those brooding dark oak refectory tables and court cupboards of the Tudor period.

Tudor rooms, unlike 1920s chic ones, should have the dark green painted in a dead flat oil which is then lightly waxed. Eighteenth-century walls may be dragged, scumbled and combed, for this, along with pea green, was the smart 18th-century alternative to wallpaper.

Pale but strong jade and grass green are more lively and work well in modern spaces without architectural detailing. These colours, too, make extremely fine emphasis points set against a darker (or lighter) shade of green. Take a dark wall and put a jade Chinese sculpture against it – carefully lit to show its translucence – and you have immediate impact. Use a grass green Venetian bottle or quilt and put it in front of the palest green wall to the same effect.

Top left **A serious, working kitchen has a cool mint background to offer calm amidst pots and crockery. Disciplined colours and objects minimize clutter.**

Top right **Because the floor, carpet, table and walls are all in shades of cream and brown, the green paintwork** and cabinet, and the green chairs, seem to base the room on a green palette.

Above **Baize-coloured walls – a favourite 19th-century art gallery colour – are used as a backdrop. The truly clever note, however, is to put the large, mint green sofa directly below.**

GREEN IN COMBINATION We are used to seeing green in combination with many colours all around us: herbaceous borders against lawns, parks alongside multi-coloured buildings.

Green is the colour you should use as a base if you want a lively, busy room using a multiplicity of colours. If you take the most frenetic of florals, combining every colour of the spectrum, and put it against a green background, your eye will be happy. I don't particularly recommend such busy fabrics, but if that's your choice pick green as the background.

For this reason, I like green in areas which are naturally busy. In the kitchen, for example, green copes calmly with any violent shade, from a string of red peppers to those truly hideous packets of cereals. You can even test the green walls by piling plums, limes or tomatoes in bowls in the foreground.

Another area suited to green is a library, whether one of those huge formal affairs where the book stacks need to be numbered or just a section of a room filled with books. Once again, the books provide masses of mixed and jittery colours which need to be pulled together with a calm base.

Above **Green has great affinity with warm wood furniture and floors, and is used on planked walls in this 17th-century house. White turns up in stripes and checks. The overscaled mouldings around the doors and the woodwork are also pure, matt white.**

Left **Though this kitchen is clearly inspired by the colours and textures of Morocco, it is vague enough to be anywhere – or anywhere that needs** a cool, breezy atmosphere. **The green of the woodwork is cleverly combined with greeny blue tiles and a turquoise chimneypiece.**

Yet another busy area is the main entrance hall and green makes a fine contribution to this, especially if it can be chosen to echo whatever greenery is outside. If you are lucky enough to have a fine view or garden (and to keep the front door open in good weather), arrange the green to emphasize the view beyond. And arrange your garden so that its glories can be seen from within. No doubt, too, your hall will be full of parcels, hats, sticks and umbrellas and so will again be helped by green's soothing properties.

Like blue, green has a natural affinity with white, and the combination is especially suited to conservatories, ferneries, garden rooms and other spaces which open onto the garden. Use it, too, for outside furniture.

Most impressive of all are the true emerald and malachite greens which were both used for those Imperial Russian rooms of the 18th century. These regal colours make a fine background for startling antiques or family portraits.

Opposite right **The soft mint ice painted on the cupboards of a simple country kitchen is hardly challenged by the silver handles and fittings, nor by the natural wood of the worktop, the floor and various baskets on show. This allows the smallest touches of red, in the tea towel and shelf edging, to contrast with the green.**

Above **Greens combined with blues, if chosen well, are casual in approach. None more casual than in this coastal American holiday-home kitchen furnished with flea-market finds.**

COLOUR CONTROL

Blue comes in two distinct varieties. One has a strong red presence, from cobalt to mauve to Saxe blue and lavender. The other has a green-yellow bias, including Prussian blue, Chinese blue and aquamarine. The two don't get on together. Red-toned blues are warm and sophisticated, while the green end of the colour is casual, maritime and, if not treated carefully, rather cold. Both look excellent with white, and more subtle with their own shades of grey (red-toned or green-toned). Red is best avoided – the two strong primaries will shout at each other – while the pastels inevitably look mimsy together.

Green is extremely versatile. At one end of its spectrum is bright, zingy lime. At the other is deep, rich malachite. Choose lime for country schemes, conservatories and light kitchens, where it teams well with white, sky blue and, in controlled amounts, scarlet. Emerald and malachite add grandeur to portrait-hung rooms, imposing halls and large drawing rooms. These colours are at ease with exotic woods such as ebony and rosewood, with oriental rugs and Chinese antiques. In between, there's a whole range of olives, sages and lavender greens, all with hints of grey and black. These subtle colours are as much at home in a modern warehouse as in a cottage. They are the perfect foil for strong indigo, lacquer red or burnt orange.

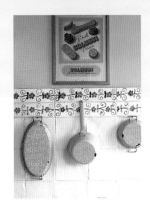

- Blue and white objects, from china to linen tea towels, can help to coordinate a scheme.

- To calm the whole, add black, grey or yellow, as paint or found objects such as pebbles.

- Metallic shades of silver look wonderful with blue: silver frames, steel banisters, iron buckets.

- Blond wood – in beech kitchen tables, pine floors, unpainted doors – mixes well with blue.

- Blue responds to geometric patterns such as two-tone wide stripes and gingham.

- It is also effective on painted furniture such as Swedish Gustavian or Shaker.

- Dark green walls provide a stunning background for paintings, especially hefty oils.

- Green can be a cold shade. Work it with warmer colours such as coral or rosy beige.

- Avoid green gloss on walls, mantelpieces or doors. Matt and eggshell work much better.

- The grey-greens – sage, olive and celadon – are ideal for painted furniture.

- Bright green patterns on a white ground freshen a dull area. Use for curtains, upholstery.

- Take bunches of leaves to put in a vase. There is a huge variety of shapes, textures and tones.

yellows

Yellow, the friendliest colour in the spectrum, brings warmth and light. It's also versatile: it can be grand but never intimidating, cosy but never sickly sweet.

Yellow is one of the most approachable colours – perhaps because it's capable of extraordinary variations and because, at its deepest and strongest, it never gets dark. It has, however, frequently been misused. Goethe was at fault, I think, when he suggested that it gave sunlight where there was none. As a consequence, yellow was often used in the dingiest, pokiest and darkest rooms of the house.

Robert Adam put yellow to work in all its classical glory. Teamed with the sharpest of white detailing, strong yellows – of several different shades if

Right **A single bright yellow dominates this countrified room, strongly contrasted with brilliant white cupboard doors and the painted fireplace. The colour is only used here.**

Left **Yellow has a strong presence in this living room in Milan, but it is a colour which can cope with both the hot summers and cold winters of northern Italy. Teaming it with gold and crimson makes for a rich effect.**

Above **Another grand room is relaxed with a dull ochre yellow, helpfully teamed with sharp white. The colours of the furniture and objects come from the same muted palette.**

need be – proved perfect for his grandest schemes. Even when soaring 20 feet up in a grand entrance hall, yellow is never oppressive and that is its secret. It's also a helpful colour, even in huge areas, because it intensifies much less than reds or blues – so is good on narrow stairways and in small spaces.

I would therefore use yellow for the grander rooms and those where you want to relax. It is equally satisfactory in town or country because it is associated both with classical 18th-century design and with rural cornfields and thatch. It's for living rooms and kitchens, for important halls and stairways. It's lovely in a generous bedroom and, because it is friendly, in children's rooms.

Yellow is always warm, but the redder the mix, the warmer it gets. I find the eggier end of the spectrum difficult to work with and always pick the sharper, citrus tones of the greener yellows. These are brighter and fresher but less cosy.

As a downside, yellow has to be carefully teamed with other colours. It's excellent with white and grey, it works well with wood and neutrals, but with red it needs to be carefully controlled, as it does with blue. A bright scarlet

Above right **This airy room shows how easy yellow is to live with – cheerful, light and unthreatening. The overscaled gingham curtains bring the various tones in the room together.**

Below **Bright scarlet makes a surprisingly good mix with soft yellow, adding pizzazz to a scheme which would otherwise be bland.**

Above and right **Two yellows combine in this kitchen: the walls are soft mustardy orange and the cupboards a clear bright yellow. A stripe of white tiles keeps them distinct.**

Far right **This corner shows how to make colours work for you. Brilliant yellow paintwork is combined with silvery equipment: bin, shovel and enamel jug. Cheap and very clever.**

While I hate the idea of green in a bathroom, yellow is a happy choice because it makes you instantly feel warm and welcome in combination with white baths, towels and washbasins.

is fine with yellow – one of the most dramatic rooms I ever saw had chrome yellow walls and scarlet silk curtains – but with crimson it is deadly.

Because of its friendliness and versatility, yellow is the perfect practical colour. It is one of the favourite shades for decorating a child's room because of its sunny character and ability to swallow clutter, even the primary-hued clutter of most children's toys.

Green, of course, has this same ability but is less cheerful. Thus yellow is a prime candidate for a kitchen. Used on walls, woodwork or cupboards, it has a natural connection with the whites of cookers and fridges and the silvers and greys of steel and aluminium pans with their black handles.

Conversely, warm yellow is probably not a good choice in warm rooms or warm countries except where it is used in small quantities for those brilliantly lively mixes of tropical colour. I find, when in a different country, it's worth looking at what the locals do, for they will have had years of experience in making the decor work with the climate.

The lime end of the yellow range appears in many Mediterranean schemes and is both cool and brilliant enough to ease the heat and light of a southern summer. The same goes for humid regions where the citrus shades of lemon, grapefruit and lime recall cool groves and orange-blossom scent.

Below left **Yellow is a perfect colour for children's rooms because it is cheerful, light and willing to team with other primary colours. This is evident in this charming bunk area, where a series of strong scarlets – cushion, toys, clothes – and a chair of acid lime green look wonderfully fresh. Several shades of yellow are included and there's even an old family portrait thrown in.**

Below right **This toy-filled bathroom has the benefit of overhead windows, which makes the citrus yellow especially sunny. The simplicity of the colour scheme means the toys are fun, not clutter.**

YELLOW IN COMBINATION
Mixtures based on yellow can be striking: yellow is both a dramatic hue and one which is improved by strong contrasts.

Yellow, though a primary colour, is lighter and more flexible than red and blue. As you can see on this page, it sings when juxtaposed with a saturated scarlet. Yellow and blue is a great combination because it is so lively, yet so friendly.

The trick when using these strong characters is to limit the amount of pattern to a minimum and to be quite clear which of the two colours is boss. In most schemes, I would plump for the yellow because it is not so domineering, teamed with solid blocks of scarlet or cobalt. It's possible, with a very controlled scheme, to add more stinging colours like lime, orange or shocking pink to the mix. Think tropical here.

Another dramatic mixture is to team yellow with black. This again needs great care, otherwise the room will look like a wasp. But black-and-white curtains, whether in classical patterns or geometrics, look good, as does severe modern furniture, perhaps with monochrome prints. Any strong or pale yellow is suitable here.

Above **Breaking all the rules, this living area combines all three primaries, with the brilliant scarlet sofa set against bright yellow walls. The blue cushion adds the third dimension.**

Right **The cool green of sandblasted glass turns up in a city apartment teamed with mingled shades of yellow to create a lively, springlike feeling.**

More games with strong colours turn up in another city apartment – these mixes are definitely urban combinations. Orange and shades of different bright, light yellows are used to zone different areas. White draws the eye beyond.

oranges

Don't be afraid of orange. Despite the regular bad press it gets in the garden (often rightly), indoors it can be a much gentler beast, easily tamed.

One way to control your doubts when working with this colour is not to call it orange. Think of it variously as terracotta, Seville, coral and cornelian. There, that's better. At once it becomes a lively, warm colour which is capable of adapting itself to many different international styles. It features greatly in the tropics (one dark orange was once known as Indian red) and many 'ethnic' rooms will benefit from knocked-back orange walls against which can be arranged wooden Buddhas, brass elephants, ornate mirrors and colourful textiles.

In another guise, many Chinese lacquers veer more to soft orange than the usual red. This complex colour, best achieved by layers and layers painted

Above If you live in Marrakesh, then it makes sense to take advantage of the predominant colour – orange in all its forms – and the wealth of objects and antiques which can be found to suit it. The earthy orange walls are a background to all shades of the orange register, from pale cream to dark terracotta.

Right **Orange, slightly dulled, takes on a suggestion of the earth tone sienna, and therefore is ideal in Mediterranean rooms. Here, it's Provence.**

on a wall and combining both opaque and transparent finishes, becomes a wonderful backdrop for Chinese furniture, itself lacquered red and brown or in dark, exotic hardwoods. Since Chinese furniture is not only fashionable but available, these decorative schemes are very of the moment.

Another country which can be evoked by the use of orange walls is Italy, whether the interior of a rustic farmhouse set among the terracotta olive groves of Tuscany or the crumbling palaces of Sicily surrounded by brilliant light and orange groves.

I find if a colour looks right in a landscape, then the house in that setting will also benefit from these colours. And oranges, terracottas, Suffolk pink,

Above and below **The strong light of Morocco and the large, though veiled, windows and doors allow the intensity of orange to provide a curiously cool haven from the heat. This may be because the colour is natural to the country's landscape and buildings, where terracotta is constantly used for flooring and ornament.**

Above **Orange, which is here knocked back to a warm amber, has a natural affinity with dark and pale greys. This corner of a living room, its walls unadorned with pictures, relies on the contrast of an intriguing dark stone floor patterned with inset cobbles. Between the two, the white skirting board keeps the lines clean.**

Above right **Though orange is not considered to be either peaceful or calm, this study area achieves both. How? We have nothing here but a single, matt deep orange wall against which is set heavily grained rosewood furniture which almost disappears into it. For the rest, the carpet and ceiling are plain white with light flooding in from the window and globe lamp. The strongest statement in the room is the poised stalk desk lamp.**

raw sienna and, of course, brick, are all shades which are used on house exteriors from Umbria to East Anglia, the Hebrides to Florida.

If you have a house which is painted outside, it's a neat idea to bring some of the colour indoors, but used a shade lighter or darker. Therefore, a typical Tuscan terracotta exterior will change to a coral indoors which casts shadows back to terracotta; an apricot lime wash on a country cottage in East Anglia will be translated into a dull blood orange in a warming dining kitchen with a cream Aga; a townhouse of dark brick will have halls and landings all painted the soft pink of raw plaster.

You can use the same trick with soft furnishings and add texture, too: team coral with the palest baby blush curtains or with unbleached cream linen; add brilliant orange slubbed-silk cushions to a scheme based on pale yellow or cream; or take the ultimate luxury of matt velvet or damask fabric in the deepest dark orange you can find and pose it with strong orange walls in a hall or mother-of-pearl in a sunny drawing room.

Like yellow, orange is a friendly colour in practical areas like kitchens and children's playrooms (though strong orange is a bit lively for a bedroom). It is friendly and warm and has some of yellow's ability to overcome clutter.

However, like red, its other component, this is a colour which demands attention. It comes forward to the eye and bullies other colours into submission (which is why gardeners hate it). So use it with discretion if you want glamour allied with calm, or take full advantage of its natural drama.

You need to be brave to use orange as a primary colour –
but it can be done if carefully balanced by other shades.

Above left **Though the orange of this kitchen's walls appears to be the strongest colour in the room, the effect is to show up the various implements and hood because the black tiling makes such a contrast. The steel of the chimney and the casually displayed utensils create the pattern.**

Above right **This is an even stronger orange statement because the colour is more intense, the paint shiny and even the ceiling coloured in with the walls. Yet it is a rural scheme, largely because of the old table and flagged floor.**

Right **Complementary orange and bright blue are teamed in exact quantities so that this small bathroom is not overpowered by their combination. A line of blue tiles calms the floor.**

Above **The calm friendliness of cream is enlivened in this corner by a slash of strong orange. The creams, from off-white to ochre and tan, ease the surprise on the eye.**

ORANGE IN COMBINATION Orange is surprisingly helpful mixed with other colours. It's just a matter of ensuring their values do not collide and scream.

The first combination to work with orange are the neutrals. Many natural timbers and fabrics are basically very knocked-back oranges, so they will look comfortable together.

This goes for all the cream, bone, stone and tan colours. Most of these colours also work very well together so it's possible to create a scheme using an amalgam of white, string and drab, with natural wood floors and furniture, then adding a single note of orange. This can be a strident pure orange or a dulled terracotta or brick. All look good.

The same goes for the range of greys, though white or black are best combined with a softened shade of orange. And reds, blues and yellows can work if you restrict them severely.

Left **The palest orange walls imaginable house adventurous pieces in this New York apartment. The colour is repeated in the cushions, glass, lampshades and large abstract picture.**

This page **The natural calm of blond wood is always a calming note in strong colour treatments. Here yellow, cream and bright orange tones make a warm, modern room.**

golds

Gold in decorating is not just the metal – though that certainly has its place – but also that shade which hovers between orange and yellow and brown.

Metallic gold is, in every way, wonderful to work with, even though it really must be the genuine article, laid on in minute slivers and veneers as gold leaf. Do not even think about cheaper paints. 'Gold' in decorating also takes in various other metallic, glittering colours: brass, which is shinier and, well, more brassy; light bronzes, which tend towards a darker brown; and old gold, which is when the metal has lost its shine through age and patina.

Even King Midas would have, I imagine, drawn the line at having a whole room leafed in gold. Impossible to live with – like an entire room of mirrors –

Below **Large corner windows let in enough light to make this golden room possible. Heavily patterned walls and 'leopard' rug still let the strong gold-leaf effect of the painting take charge.**

and it's so showy. Used in small quantities on frames, in furniture, ormolu or to enhance 18th-century panelling, gold is both glamorous and elegant. Gold also looks fine with other metals – silver, aluminium, mercury and dull zinc.

Where the trouble comes is with gold used as a colour rather than a metal. 'Gold' and old gold in paintwork can be very murky and eggy, having both the unsatisfactory qualities of yellow and brown. But, like orange, it will be happy beside the brown, cream and stone range of neutrals where, if you are clever, it will begin to look like very old, faded and genuine gold. It's therefore an idea to use it, distressed, on antiqued furniture backed by tan, or to pick very light wooden furniture, like birch and ash, to front it. Another trick is to use gold in translucent fabrics or in areas which get strong sunlight where, once again, the base paint will look gilded.

The same trick will work using gold under a strong spot at night. An idea here is to use an old goldsmith's technique and to paint an Indian red or darker undercoat below the gold and then distress it slightly. This gives an impression of applied gold leaf. You can take this even further by painting the gold on in rectangles as though applied in gold-leaf form.

Gold walls are also an attractive background to gilded objects such as Eastern statues, candelabra and glittery hangings.

Top left **A mix of timber, tan leather, tiles and soft sienna walls and curtains makes a golden room.**

Top right **Gold leaf has been used on the walls of a Manhattan apartment – a statement which needs strong accessories. The African bench and exotic hangings and screen provide just that.**

Above **Gold is hinted at in this small room by using it as a colour (not a metal) in the embroidery of the hangings. A strip of fabric on the bed brings in gold's familiar, a strong scarlet.**

GOLD IN COMBINATION Schemes in which gold is the key colour are hard to pull off, but combining gold with other colours is easy.

One reason is that while gold in large areas can be dingy, in small quantities (and treated right) its ponderousness changes to a theatrical solidity. For a start, you can use the real thing: if diamonds are a girl's best friend, then gold is the same for a room. And don't just stick with the 24-carat stuff: add brass, silver, mercury and bronze, for these will provide a handsome backing that allows even a small amount of gold to glitter in sunlight or candlelight.

Even if you can't – or won't – go for gold, then you can use the colour for walls and fabrics but lightened by mixing it with other good colours. Old gold, which is virtually a light olive green, is splendid allied with black – as, indeed, are any shades in the gold range. Olive gold is a neutral which helps emphasize the blackness around it.

Gold, too, has an affinity with all the browns, from the deepest ebony off-black to terracotta and conker brown. Tan furniture, used by the Arts and Crafts designers, can be set against walls which are either darker or lighter,

Left **A natural antique
marble basin of creamy
yellow sits against a wall
of crackle-glazed red and
gold which is both ancient
in feeling and luxurious
in atmosphere.**

Below **Gold touches on soft
beige walls create a rich
effect in this Moroccan
hammam – a steam bath
with ventilated ceiling.**

while in modern schemes it can be placed against those
fashionable soft French limestone floors or pale travertine
marbles. In both cases, if the floor of a room is as pale as
possible, darker old golds on the walls will be less heavy.

Golds are much used in Eastern decoration, so if you want
to deck your rooms with mirrored tapestries, carved stone
deities or tables made from Indian temple doors, a very dull
version of gold will make a good background. Think of it as
a soft ironstone. Similarly, various 18th-century background
colours are knocked-back golds – drab, mouse's back, wet
sand, biscuit and fawn are all examples.

If you don't believe me, look carefully at how an artist creates
an impression of gold from plain oil paints. There's a Lely lady
in London's National Portrait Gallery dressed in a luscious
golden satin gown. Lely has achieved its lustre using a palette
of tans, egg yellows, ochres and pale creams against a stormy
background of deep brown trees. So to make gold impressive
in a room, copy a swagger portraitist at his most boastful.

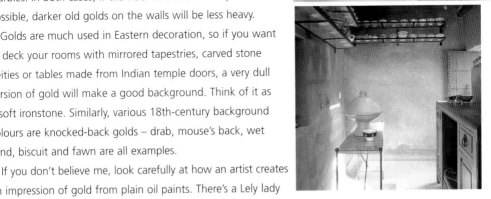

Above **Bright golden walls
create an exciting kitchen,
with ornamental
couscousière, in the same
house featured top left.**

Yellow is the gentlest of the primaries and
one which never becomes dark or threatening.
Though it's wrong to use it to 'create' sunlight in
dark rooms (it doesn't work and has given yellow
a bad image), this is a cheering and warming
colour. As with most colours, the two extremes
of the yellow spectrum should be kept firmly
apart: egg and lime is not a good combination,
but either one can be used both in the grandest
or simplest of schemes. It was a favourite in high
Georgian state rooms with white plasterwork
and is just as favoured in cluttered children's play
areas for its ability to live easily with strong
primaries as well as most neutrals. Make use of
it also in cluttered halls, busy offices and libraries.

Oranges and golds Assertive orange
strikes fear into the hearts of decorators. But
decorators can discipline orange by softening it
to coral, brick or terracotta. When planning an
orange scheme, therefore, think in gentler colour
names. Gold also needs to be looked at in a
different way. The pure metal is no problem, for
its gleam softens its colour, but large areas of
paint won't work unless the hue is dulled. Think
of a soft olive, tan or cream when working with
gold and, if you can't dull the overall colour,
reduce its impact with plenty of near-gold shades.

- Yellow is good for very large rooms and high-ceilinged staircases and halls because, though strong, it never threatens.

- Yellow will intensify in narrow spaces and strengthen the colour. So it's good in corridors.

- Yellow, though warm, is a dramatic colour when teamed with other primaries like scarlet or with black or dark brown.

- Bedrooms in yellow are at once relaxing and cheering. Yellow mixes well with white linen and is neither consciously masculine nor feminine.

- When muted with white, yellow becomes a virtual neutral and is good for woodwork, painted furniture or rough upholstery.

- Yellow is, of course, common in flowers. Use large bunches to freshen a dark or winter room.

- Dulled oranges are landscape colours. Use earth shades inside, but change their tone.

- Orange is good with primaries and other strong colours in unfussy rooms.

- Pure orange in small doses grabs attention. It's good on shiny surfaces such as silk or glass.

- When using gold, try to treat it like real gold leaf. Add an undercoat of red or dark tan before painting a distressed finish. Or apply the paint in small rectangles, the size of a gold-leaf book.

- Gold (the paint) is a good background for gold (the metal). Put gilded frames and statues against an old gold background.

reds

Red is the most difficult colour to use. It is both intense and gloomy, reduces space and bounces from the walls. But, used well, red can be dramatic.

Red signals danger and that's exactly what it means in decorative terms. It is the strongest of colours, and the more red you use the more it intensifies. Strong red walls turn white paintwork pink. They crowd in on you, enclosing you as though in a womb. Red is also a clichéd colour, especially in dining rooms, where it rarely works, and libraries, which it suits better. The positive side is that, subtly used, its shades and tints are powerful and memorable.

Below **It is the clever use of grey and black in the ornaments and metal tub which gives this red room its charm. Everything from the framed photo and the vases to the pussy-willow sprigs is considered. Note the lack of white paint.**

There are several ways to tackle the colour. Use it in rooms where there is little wall space because of shelves, windows or cupboards – or in enormous spaces, such as warehouses, lofts or billiard rooms, where you want to bring the walls forward and make things a bit warmer.

If you are designing a room with red walls, pick your colour carefully. The brighter scarlets can be too dramatic for comfort, while the deep crimsons are gloomy. I would pick the subtle brown-red of old Chinese lacquer.

Because red is such a thug, not only with other colours but with itself, it asks for the most simple of treatments. It is not, for example, a good idea to use a large palette of colours in a basically red room: this not only looks messy but also dilutes the whole point of using red. You want drama, not confusion.

It is also a good idea to avoid using much white in an overpoweringly red room. As I found out, using clear scarlet

Above **It looks like an all-red bedroom, but its window, white dado and floor let the room breathe.**

Below **The matt red walls of this room were glazed with a darker shade to avoid a flat effect. Dark browns and blacks provide solidity and contrast.**

Above **Large areas of floor, window and dado mean that this apparently all-red room is anything but. The space, however, is large enough for the white to remain uncontaminated by the strong lacquer red.**

Left **Objects in the room above enforce the oriental feeling but are in duller shades of the same red.**

Far left **Strong red may cover the walls here, but not much is visible because of the books, baskets, large hanging and marble fireplace, all in a range of off-whites.**

If you are lucky enough to have a picture gallery, red is a good shade for strong oil paintings (never watercolours), and libraries are busy enough with books for the red to take second place.

up a narrow set of stairs, white turns a nasty shade of pink when used with red in confined spaces. My idea for the stairs was copied from the grand hallway and stairs of a Dublin house, which looked theatrical but stately, but I had ignored the fact that it was a large open space. Even the stairs were cantilevered and without a second wall.

Even in normal rooms – smaller than the Dublin version – white has a tendency to go pink, or else it detracts from the red because it contrasts too strongly. If I wanted pale woodwork on doors and skirtings, I would plump for a silver-grey. Equally, wood left unpainted fits the colour.

All neutrals are a possibility but the one which really suits red, especially if you are working on a deliberately dark and emphatic room, is black or off-blacks like ebony and charcoal. I wouldn't, of course, use it for the

Below left and right **This room exemplifies one of the hardest decorative feats involving colour. The uncompromising scheme works here because it uses only one single colour – a dark lacquer red on walls, shelves, furniture and floor – with bright spots of light to relieve the darkness. Even the two portraits have been picked for their dark shades. This is a night-time room for reading, entertaining and – oddly enough – relaxing.**

Among the National Trust colours is one called Fox Red, described as 'one of the clearest reds possible using finest burnt-earth pigments', but it is actually more like brick or terracotta.

woodwork but certainly for objects, furniture and picture frames. Groups of monochrome photographs are excellent on red walls, while good modern furniture, especially in black leather, will be equal to the force of the walls.

Deep reds of the lacquer variety are excellent in 16th- and 17th-century rooms, which were always sombre and ill lit. The colour, much used during that period, well suits the dark oak furniture of the Tudors and the foxy red grain of walnut which succeeded it in fashion.

Among the famous National Trust paint colours is one called Fox Red. It is perfect for these early houses. Later Trust colours include Etruscan Red, which was much used by the Romans but became fashionable in Europe after the discovery of Pompeii, where it was often the main background for the town's amazing murals. Even stronger are Eating Room Red, Book Room Red and Picture Gallery Red – the latter copied from Attingham Park.

These names say a lot about where, historically, strong red was most used but I would certainly hesitate to put Eating Room Red in an eating room, unless it was near ballroom-sized and filled with family portraits.

Above left **A beautifully controlled bedroom collects a score of reds together, but the whole is made subservient to a heavily carved Portuguese half tester bed.**

Above right **A textured red quilt matches the knocked-back walls of a bedroom and the whole is teamed with shades of olive.**

Opposite **These walls, distressed to look like raw plaster, are the perfect complement to a collection of antique textiles, all of them dyed various shades of madder.**

This page **White, scarlet and black** – perhaps the strongest combination of colours available to a designer – are combined in this Manhattan apartment. What's more, the owners have furnished it with strong designer furniture such as Mies van der Rohe red leather chairs from 1929 and a quantity of 20th-century collectors' pieces of glass and china. The darker red cubed rug and the blank white walls provide an individual background.

Opposite **Taking inspiration** from an anemone on the table, the strong reds of this kitchen are mixed with black for the worktops, niches and an area just below the ceiling. Then steel blue, varying from soft hints in glass bottles and highlights on steel equipment to sea blue crockery, is added to the mix. Because both black and steel are neutral (and the soft blue is unthreatening), the red is kept under control.

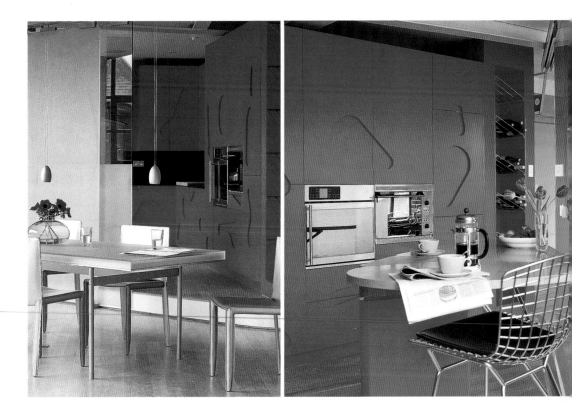

RED IN COMBINATION Even mixed with other colours, red is no pushover unless used in small quantities. Red grabs attention, which can throw out the balance of what you want to achieve.

This colour is fine for focal points and to bring the eye to where you want it. A single vase of brilliant scarlet dahlias or tulips, for instance, will attract attention and, if there are other less forceful reds in the area, they will be emphasized too.

So, if you have paintings with touches of red, a set of madder toile cushions or a paisley throw, add a brilliant vase of flowers and you'll be surprised what a difference it makes.

Another great mixer with strong red is silver (not gold, which tends to be pompous except in grand areas). Silver and allied metals such as zinc, brushed steel and aluminium are at once cool and strong and, unlike white, they do not get corrupted by the strong red. Indeed, metal furniture, screens and objects seem to diffuse the heat of red and almost put it in the background. The same applies to large mirrors.

pinks and lilacs

I do wish that pink did not have such cumbersome baggage to carry: it's seen as the colour of sherbet, spoiled little girls and Barbara Cartland's dresses.

Let's therefore think Schiaparelli, who famously invented (or at least used) shocking pink, a colour so vibrant that it shocked you into attention. It is roughly the same brilliant pink at the blue end of the range that Diana Vreeland said is the navy blue of India. She meant that, in the fierce light of that country's sun and against its other common colours like lime green and ultramarine, pink was as basic as navy is to the cold north.

Shocking pink is similar to cerise, in theory the colour of a cherry but in fact much more blue. A tint paler is rose, a favourite with 20th-century country-house owners and, as such, something of a cliché. However, combine rose with other pinks and you will achieve an extraordinarily modern effect.

Top and above **This room is decorated in a series of pinks which intensify each other. The scheme mixes textures, from the shiny curtains to the woven cloth pattern, and teams them exotically with gold.**

Above left and right
Combinations of pink and lilac, such as this bedroom and tablescape, can be made quickly with flowers, hangings, a throw or cloth, along with piles of books and even feathers.

Left **This large drawing room is decorated in many different pinks, all from the same palette. Three are combined for the walls, while the curtains are brighter and the rug in a deeper shade.**

So, pinks are by no means as mimsy as we make out. Put together cerise, shocking pink and rose and you will have a room which narrowly avoids clashes – but the narrowness of the escape adds to the thrill. More calmly, you can take rose as the strongest colour of the mix and add pale mother-of-pearl and a hint of sherbet. It will still work and looks especially good with plenty of pattern.

But pinks and lilacs are the range of colours which can produce seriously awful clashes – only nature can avoid a clash, just as she avoids a vacuum. The problem is that the yellow end of the red spectrum looks appalling when teamed with the blue end. Clashing is just as bad among the softened pinks, perhaps because it's not so easy to define a paler colour.

It's thus highly important that you work with a colour board here or, better still, with a corner of the designated room. Pinks, like reds, have a habit of intensifying when used together, so what looks fine when decided upon in small swatches can become alarmingly awful in large.

Beware – this colour range can produce some terrible clashes. Think tangerine and lilac, or the old school tie of puce and egg.

Above The lilac used on the walls, coving and ceiling of this attic bedroom is so soft it appears almost off-white, warmed to sugar-almond strength by gaining intensity in the shadows. Strong light, the simple bed linen and the distressed wardrobe give the room space and charm.

I would recommend experimenting with several areas of the room – one part in strong light by the window, another in a darker corner. Paint each with your chosen shades of pink or lilac in at least a square metre. Then add a woodwork colour (grey is good, as are the beige neutrals). Finally, put as much fabric as you can get as a sample alongside. Try the mixture out both in day and electric light, because these colours can change greatly by night. If you are the slightest bit unsure, keep changing the mix.

Is the pink too orange, too strong, too sugary? Are you using it in too large quantities or mixing too many shades and tints? Or perhaps you

could use more variations because the more and lighter areas you can create, the more the strongest hue will be tamed.

Once you have the colour's measure, pink and its bluer sister, lilac, are endlessly adaptable. If you consider the variations in the petals of a single deep pink rose or a pearly oriental poppy, you will see how much you can play about with it. The point is that each variation, from dullest rose madder to nacreous pearl, must be of exactly the same blue or yellow mix.

When you look at historic houses, pink was virtually never used unless it was a pale terracotta (though Ointment Pink, painted on hall and staircase at Ireland's Castle Coole, was famously described by the previous owner as Germolene, after a particularly colourful rub). This was largely because it was so hard to create from available pigments until mauve, magenta and shocking pink dyes were invented in the mid-19th century. So this range is one of the most truly modern available and should be used with gusto and verve.

This page **Steel has a natural affinity with the lilac end of the blue range. This is perfect for kitchen areas with lots of steel equipment. Here metallic blue chairs, steel handles, lights, storage and equipment take the idea to its limits. Note, however, the slash of pale olive above the cabinets.**

PINK AND LILAC IN COMBINATION   Pink and lilac often live well together, but mixing them with other shades can be difficult.

Above left **This bedroom plays the gamut of lavender blue, from the pale floor to the vibrant lavenders on the bed. The owner has almost done away with decorations.**

Above right **Don't be frightened of lilac and mauve. Call them hyacinth or lavender to make them more friendly, as in this charming room which intermingles the colour of the walls with other sugar-almond shades.**

White is not the answer here because it reacts by losing its identity. My view is that the best neutral to mingle with lilac or pink is a bluey grey. It doesn't really matter how dark or light the grey, for it's very amenable. Charcoal makes a fine contrast either to a pale, dreamy lilac or a shocking pink – but so does the palest silver-grey. Black is another successful mixer.

Take grey further into the blue realm and it should be happy, especially with lilac and mauve, though the mixture will be recessive and cold. Warm up the lilac by adding a tan at the grey end of its spectrum – pale limed timber boards or furniture will be fine, but take care with a conker brown.

Then there are the metals: all the silvers and steels look terrific here, though once again cold. Use gold, bronze and brass in small quantities only. My tip is to stick with a mix of pink and lilac backed by a single neutral grey.

This cool living room, despite its combination of lilacs and dull pinks, relies on strong shapes and a neutral grey floor for its effect. The textures here vary from gleaming leather and silk to matt upholstery.

purples

Purple is the colour of majesty – largely because it was so expensive to create. It also signifies mourning and princes of the church, so treat it with reverence.

This page and opposite **These three shots of Michelle Halard's French dining room show what purple can become in the hands of a skilled designer. She has used it with a range of soft beiges, greiges and orangey tans found in the ornaments, sketches and picture mounts, with touches of olive green in the painted furniture. More bravely, she has added acid yellow by laying the table with bright crockery. This could, of course, easily be varied.**

On this page we have found a rare person who wants to paint rooms an unrelieved purple and, you must admit, the results are pretty Gothic. But then there is a school of designers who like to evoke a touch of horror film in a room (I promise you). Curiously, if you can cast aside the connotations, purple isn't all that impossible. Think of it as a reddish navy blue and treat it as an imposing, unconventional shade. Keep it for night-time rooms, from dining areas to bedrooms, where it is surprisingly cosy.

PURPLE IN COMBINATION   Mixed with other colours, purple loses its daunting majesty to become a modern spice for stark spaces.

Perhaps because none of this range of hues – magenta, violet and purple – was much used before the mid-19th century and because, when the Victorians got their hands on them, they were deployed with sombre gloom, we underestimate their powers. I do believe that it's helpful when considering unconventional shades to give them different names, and this is especially the case with magenta and purple. Think of dark clematis, pansy or black hollyhock – all greatly loved by gardeners for their near-black effect.

A truly dark purple comes nearer black than either midnight blue or darkest green, because its basis only hints at colour. A dark purple can vary from near ebony brown to almost navy, and these shades should be treated differently. Both, of course, look luxurious teamed with pure white or with silver and steel. Grey is a great neutral at the blue end, and stone or bone the perfect foil at the brown end. So are faux furs and other textured browns and near-blacks.

But purple can also be combined with the most surprising and brilliant colours. Here we show it with orange and violet and it works because the purple is so dark as to be neutral. Yet, if black were substituted, the orange would be shown as coarse and unpleasant. In the same room, a good strong clear blue – Chinese blue or cerulean – could replace the orange with the same vibrant effect, as could a simple grass green, a touch bluer than lime.

Because black is rarely found in nature in its true form, most of the dark, recessive shades are, in fact, deep purple and these are used by gardeners to add background weight to colourful borders. Anyone who longs to use purple could with advantage visit gardens famous for their use of colour – Great Dixter, for example, or Hadspen – or could look at the work of modern horticulturalists at garden shows for some idea of purple's properties.

Above left **Purple is beautiful in bedrooms because it feels extremely luxurious and cosy. It is the colour of warm nights. Here a series of purples in shiny and matt fabrics adorns a simple neutral bedroom. Even the calla lilies in vases are just right for the room.**

Above right **You don't have to leave a half-full wineglass to get the idea that this pile of cushions is based on wine colours, from deep burgundy to claret and rosé. It's all contrasted with a soothing stony grey.**

When you work with deep and strong colours or with complementaries – as in this small apartment – it's a good idea to think about texture as variation. The deep purple of the far wall, for example, was created by rubbing purple pigment into wet plaster, which gave it a velvety depth. Given one entire wall of glass, the owner has added stinging orange velvet and shocking pink silk cushions.

COLOUR CONTROL

Red is a bullying and pompous colour and should never be used in clichéd positions such as formal dining rooms. It also tends to be a night-time colour, working successfully in rooms used for lounging or entertaining after dark. All-red schemes are very rare – but if you see one that works, note exactly the colour and context for future reference. Red in combination, especially used slightly and deftly, is extremely useful. A single vase of scarlet flowers will stand out in a neutral or dark room and have the added effect of focusing on other reds nearby. Reds have a great tendency to clash – more so than any other colour – and the two different ends of its spectrum, the yellow and blue, should be strictly segregated.

Pinks, lilacs and purples No one invented a clear range of purples, pinks and lilacs until the mid-19th century, so they were rarely used historically. That makes the range one of the most modern and one we have yet to appreciate fully. Drop the majesty of Imperial Purple and think of these colours as black pansy, blueberry and lavender, with 20th-century bright pink thrown in. These colours respond to shock treatment; they can be teamed with brilliant orange, ebony brown and malachite green as long as the two are not of the same tone. In general, dark purple is as adaptable as midnight blue, and lilac as pale blue.

- Red is a night-time, grown-up colour with a strong need to dominate. Use with extreme care.

- One of the best neutrals with all reds is a soft or dark grey. Make it blue-grey with blue-reds and brown-grey with the orange-reds.

- One of the most successful combinations with strong red is the whole range of silver metals, from steel to zinc. Large mirrors are excellent in red schemes for this reason.

- Use strong reds as accents in neutral rooms. A bunch of scarlet sweet peas will have an effect out of all proportion. A strong accent will also emphasize other, weaker reds around it.

- Avoid using bright white with a strong red. It will absorb the colour and turn a nasty pink.

- One of the most fashionable reds at present is the subtle, dull vermilion of Chinese lacquer. If you pick one strong red, make it this.

- Team shocking pink with neutrals such as grey, charcoal, black and beige, but never bright white.

- If you keep to a single hue of pink, you can mix in quantities of different shades and tints.

- Lilacs, always clear, range from strong violet to softest mother-of-pearl. Team all together.

- Dark purple is as adaptable as navy. It's excellent with white (and less clichéd) and perfectly at home with brilliant orange or pink.

- These colours should all be tried out in large areas (one square metre minimum) in dark and light spaces – and by day and in artificial light – to be absolutely sure they don't clash.

• Finding inspiration is fun. You will find that the more you keep your eyes open, the better you will see.

• Inspiration can strike at any time, so always carry a notebook and, if possible, paint swatches. Keep it all together so you don't forget crucial bits.

• I find the combinations used in borders by top garden designers and horticulturalists to be full of ideas. Visit gardens in June (the best time of year) to pick up ideas. Also buy gardening books about colour – they are just as useful as design books.

• Can't decide what colour to use? Paint everything a soft white until you get inspired.

• Add temporary objects – flowers, throws, cushions – to the plain white mix and see which suits the mood of your room.

• When you are making a colour board, add a vase of flowers in front. Look at the shades of a single rose and how the colour intensifies and deepens. Watch how a bunch of scarlet tulips will transform a white room.

• Try out your colour board in different lights – strong sun, a dull day, artificial light similar to that you have planned for the room.

• While blues and greens are inspired by the landscape, pinks and purples are less natural. Your sources of inspiration are therefore likely to be manmade – including garden flowers.

Introduction

I hope that you live with this book, get its corners dunched and its pages worn. It is intended to be your constant companion and used to the full: sketch ideas on the graph paper or write notes about colour combinations and inspirations. Fill the pockets with scraps of ribbon or paper to recall chosen colours. Then, if my lists of suppliers don't give you enough leeway, add more in the address book which follows. Keep the book by you, in a smart bag filled with swatches and snaps, as a working tool. Then, when your home is perfect, keep it to bring back memories.

notes and sketches

notes and sketches

notes and sketches

notes and sketches

favourite addresses

name

address

tel

fax

e-mail

www

name

address

tel

fax

e-mail

www

name

address

tel

fax

e-mail

www

name

address

tel

fax

e-mail

www

name

address

tel

fax

e-mail

www

name

address

tel

fax

e-mail

www

name

address

tel

fax

e-mail

www

name

address

tel

fax

e-mail

www

name

address

tel
fax
e-mail
www

name

address

tel
fax
e-mail
www

name

address

tel
fax
e-mail
www

name

address

tel
fax
e-mail
www

name

address

tel
fax
e-mail
www

name

address

tel
fax
e-mail
www

name

address

tel
fax
e-mail
www

name

address

tel
fax
e-mail
www

stockists

Akzo Nobel Woodcare
Meadow Lane
Huntingdon
Cambs PE27 4UY
Tel: 01480 496868
www.akzonobel.co.uk
Wood preservatives, stains
and varnishes.

Alice & Astrid
30 Artesian Road
London W2 5DD
Tel: 020 7985 0888
www.aliceandastrid.com
Cushions and accessories.

Alma Home
12–14 Greatorex Street
London E1 5NF
Tel: 020 7377 0762
www.almahome.co.uk
Leather and suede
furniture, wall tiles,
headboards, placemats,
sheepskin rugs and throws.

Altfield
Unit 2/22
Chelsea Harbour Design
Centre
London SW10 0XE
Tel: 020 7351 5893
www.altfield.com
Handpainted silk and
needlepoint cushions,
lamps, porcelain, screens,
Chinese wallpaper panels.

Amari Plastics
Holmes House
24–30 Baker St
Weybridge
Surrey KT13 8AU
Tel: 01932 835000
www.amariplastics.com
Coloured perspex sheets.

Bill Amberg
21–22 Chepstow Corner
London W2 4XE
Tel: 020 7727 3560
www.billamberg.com
Leather in places you never
imagined – round banister
rails, as wine racks, floor
coverings and accessories.

Anta
Fearn, Tain
Ross-shire IV20 1XW
Tel: 01862 832477
www.anta.co.uk
Reworked tartans and plaids,
carpets and Scottish pottery.

Appeal Conservatory Blinds
Freephone brochure line:
0800 9755757
www.appealblinds.com
Conservatory blinds.

Laura Ashley
P.O. Box 19
Newtown
Powys SY16 1DZ
Tel: 0871 9835999
www.lauraashley.com
Furnishing fabrics, paint
and wallpaper including
children's fabrics and
wallpapers.

**Association of Master
Upholsterers and Soft
Furnishers**
Frances Vaughan House
Q1 Capital Point Business
Centre
Capital Business Park
Parkway
Cardiff CF3 2PU
Tel: 029 2077 8918
www.upholsterers.co.uk
Where to find someone to
recover your furniture.

Atrium
Centrepoint
22–24 St Giles High Street
London WC2H 8TA
Tel: 020 7379 7288
www.atrium.ltd.uk
Simulated leather and
suede furniture, lighting.

Auro UK
Cheltenham Road
Bisley
Nr Stroud
Gloucestershire GL6 7BX
Tel: 01452 772020
www.auroorganic.co.uk
Manufacturer of organic
paints which has received
certification as a result of
an independent eco-audit.

Jonathan Avery
7–15 Church Hill Place
Morningside
Edinburgh EH10 4BE
Tel: 0131 4471000
www.jonathanavery.co.uk
Painted furniture, unfitted
freestanding kitchens and
library bookcases.

G P & J Baker Ltd
Chelsea Harbour Design
Centre
G18/19 North Dome
London SW10 0XE
Tel: 020 7351 7760
www.gpjbaker.co.uk
Curtain/upholstery fabrics.

Beauchamp Interiors
Unit 8–10, Red Rose Court
Sunnyhurst
Blackburn
Lancs BB2 1PS
Tel: 01254 668185 or
01254 689253
www. beauchamp
interiors.com
Historic wallpaper and
to commission.

Beaumont & Fletcher
261 Fulham Road
London SW3 6HY
Tel: 020 7352 5594
www.beaumontand
fletcher.com
English-style fabrics,
wallpapers, upholstered
furniture and accessories.

Bennison Fabrics
16 Holbein Place
London SW1W 8NL
Tel: 020 7730 8076
www.bennisonfabrics.com
Traditional tea-stained
fabrics and accessories.

Bentley & Spens
Tel: 020 7485 6099
(London) or 01326 341457
(Cornwall)
www.fabenglish.com
Wallcoverings, fabrics and
accessories.

**Harry Berger Cleaners
& Dyers**
25 Station Road
Cheadle Hulme
Cheshire SK8 5AF
Tel: 0161 4853421
www.harryberger.com
Colour stripping, cleaning,
dyeing and invisible
mending service.

**The Berwick Street
Cloth Shop**
14 Berwick Street
London W1F 0PP
Tel: 020 7287 2881
Wide range of fabrics and
trimmings.

The Blue Door
74 Church Road
London SW13 0DQ
Tel: 020 8748 9785
www.bluedoorbarnes.co.uk
Painted Swedish-style
furniture, textiles, lighting
and accessories.

Joanna Booth
P.O. Box 50886
London SW3 5EL
Tel: 020 7352 8998
www.joannabooth.co.uk
Antique textiles; tapestries,
tapestry cushions; advice on
textile conservation

John Boyd Textiles
Higher Flax Mills
Castle Cary
Somerset BA7 7DY
Tel: 01963 350451
www.johnboydtextiles.co.uk
Britain's only horsehair
weavers, many colours and
textures for upholstery.

The Bradley Collection
Lion Barn
Maitland Road
Needham Market
Suffolk IP6 8NS
Tel: 0845 1187224
www.bradleycollection.co.uk
Curtain poles and finials,
both ready-made and made
to order.

**Bridge of Weir Leather
Company Ltd**
Baltic Works
Kilbarchan Road
Bridge of Weir
Renfrewshire PA11 3RH
Tel: 01505 612132
www.bowleather.co.uk
Upholstery leathers in
130 colours.

Bristol Blue Glass
Unit 7
Whitby Road
Bristol BS4 3QF
Tel: 0117 9720818
www.bristol-glass.co.uk
Handblown ultramarine
glass in the 18th-century
manner for vases, glasses,
decanters, etc.

Brodie & Middleton
68 Drury Lane
London WC2B 5SP
Tel: 020 7836 7521
www.brodies.net
Specialist paint finishes and
theatrical supplies.

Butler's Specialized Glass
Unit 5 Phoenix Park
Chickenhall Lane
Eastleigh
Hants SO50 6PQ
Tel: 02380 653222
Coloured or laminated glass.

Byron & Byron Ltd
2–11 Chelsea Harbour
Design Centre
Chelsea Harbour
London SW10 0XE
Tel: 020 7376 7567
www.byronandbyron.com
Curtain poles and finials in
heraldic, Biedermeier and
modern styles.

Nina Campbell
9 Walton Street
London SW3 2JD
Tel: 020 7225 1011
www.ninacampbell.com
Wallcoverings, fabrics and
accessories.

Manuel Canovas
110 Fulham Road
London SW3 6HU
Tel: 020 7244 7427
www.manuelcanovas.com
Fabrics in innovative colour
mixtures including toiles.

Chalfont Cleaners & Dyers
222 Baker Street
London NW1 5RT
Tel: 020 7935 7316
Dyeing service for curtains
and loose covers – natural
fabrics only.

**Chelsea College of
Art & Design**
16 John Islip Street,
London SW1P 4JU
Tel: 020 7514 7751
www.chelsea.arts.ac.uk
1 year and 3 year courses
in interior design.

**Chelsea Harbour
Design Centre**
Chelsea Harbour
London SW10 0XF
Tel: 020 7225 9100
www.designcentrechelsea
   harbour.co.uk
Home to nearly 80 interior
design showrooms offering
the best in British and
international design. The
place to browse for ideas.

Chelsea Textiles
7 Walton Street
London SW3 2JD
Tel: 020 7584 0111
www.chelseatextiles.com
Crewelwork, needlepoint
and embroidered fabrics.

Jane Churchill Interiors
81 Pimlico Road
London SW1W 8PH
Tel: 020 7730 8564
www.janechurchillinteriors.
   com
Fabrics and historic paints,
wallpaper from top designer.

Colefax & Fowler
110 Fulham Road
London SW3 6HU
Tel: 020 7244 7427
www.colefax.com
Inventor and purveyor of
English country-house style
– furnishing fabrics,
wallpapers and trimmings.

The Conran Shop
Michelin House
81 Fulham Road
London SW3 6RD
Tel: 020 7589 7401
www.conranshop.co.uk
Terence Conran's
powerhouse of latest ideas.

L Cornelissen & Son
105 Great Russell Street
London WC1B 3RY
Tel: 020 7636 1045
ww.cornelissen.com
Professional materials for
artists, gilders plus
distempers and limewash.

Colour Supplies
2–3 Mark Road
Hemel Hempstead
Hertfordshire HP2 7BN
Tel: 01442 231261
Paints and accessories.

Couverture
188 Kensington Park Road,
London W11 2ES
Tel: 020 7229 2178
www.couverture.co.uk
Modern bed linen,
lambswool throws and
other accessories for
the home.

Cover Up Designs
The Barn
Hannington Farm
Hannington
Hants RG26 5TZ
Tel: 01635 297981
www.coverupdesigns.co.uk
Wide range of unpainted
tables, screens and stools;
soft furnishings to cover.

Craig & Rose
Unit 8 Halbeath
Industrial Estate
Crossgates Road
Halbeath, Dunfermline
Fife KY11 7EG
Tel: 01383 740011
www.craigandrose.com
Traditional paints, precious
metal metallic paints, red
oxide paint as used on
Forth Bridge.

Cuprinol
Wexham Road
Slough
Berkshire SL2 5DS
Tel: 0870 4441111
www.cuprinol.co.uk
Coloured wood stains and
varnishes for inside and out.

Custom Carpet Company
P. O. Box 167
Tadworth
Surrey KT20 6WH
Tel: 01737 830301
www.customcarpet
   company.co.uk
Individually designed,
handtufted carpets, rugs
and wallhangings in wool
or wool/silk.

Thomas Dare
Tower House
Ruthvenfield Road
Perth PH1 3UN
Tel: 01738 609000
www.thomasdare.com
Brightly coloured checked,
striped and plain fabrics
and trimmings.

Decorshades
5 Brewery Mews
Business Centre
St Johns Road
Isleworth
Middx TW7 6PH
Tel: 020 8847 1939
www.decorshades.com
Blinds and wallcoverings
made, including laminated
and processed roller blinds
and lined Roman blinds.
They laminate fabric to
paper for use as wallpaper.

Decorative Fabrics Gallery
322 Kings Road
London SW3 5UH
Tel: 020 7823 3455
www.decorativefabrics.co.uk
Showroom for G P & J
Baker, Monkwell and so on.

The Delabole Slate Company
Pengelly, Delabole
Cornwall PL33 9AZ
Tel: 01840 212242
www.delaboleslate.co.uk
Slate worktops, floors
and surfaces.

Descamps
197 Sloane Street
London SW1 9QX
Tel: 020 7235 6957
www.descamps.com
Colourful French bed linen.

Designers Guild
3 Latimer Place,
London, W10 6QT
Tel: 020 7893 7400
www.designersguild.com
Cleverly coloured fabrics
and painted furniture.

Ella Doran
Ground Floor Shop
46 Cheshire Street
London E2 6EH
Tel: 020 7613 0782
www.elladoran.co.uk
Digitally printed blinds and
tablemats with stones, fruit,
flowers or Chinese patterns.

Dulux
ICI Paints, Wexham Road
Slough
Berkshire SL2 5DS
Tel: 0870 4441111
www.dulux.co.uk
Huge colour range, plus
heritage colours, floor
and blackboard paint.

The Empty Box Company Ltd
The Old Dairy
Coomb Farm Buildings
Balchins Lane
Westcott, nr Dorking
Surrey RH4 3LE
Tel: 01306 740193
www.emptybox.co.uk
Handmade storage boxes.

Nicole Fabre Designs Ltd
Old School,
Church Lane
Stanhoe, Kings Lynn
Norfolk PE31 8QL
Tel: 01485 518200
www.nicolefabredesigns.
  com
Reproduction 18th- and
19th-century French
textiles, plain linens.

Farrow & Ball
Uddens Estate, Wimborne
Dorset BH21 7NL
Tel: 01202 876141
www.farrow-ball.com
Historic paints for indoors
and out, including
National Trust range.

Thomas Ferguson Irish Linen
54 Scarva Road
Banbridge, Co Down
Northern Ireland BT32 3QD
Tel: 028 40623491
www.fergusonsirishlinen.
  com
Irish table and bed linen.

Fibre Naturelle Ltd
Unit 3, Fleetsbridge
Business Centre
Upton Road, Poole
Dorset BH17 7AF
Tel: 01202 674090
www.fibrenaturelle.co.uk
Hand-woven furnishing
fabrics, throws and
cushions.

Fired Earth
Twyford Mill
Oxford Road, Adderbury
Oxon OX17 3SX
Tel: 01295 812088
www.firedearth.com
Floor and wall tiles, paint,
rugs, natural flooring
and fabrics.

Forbo-Nairn
P. O. Box 1, Kirkaldy
Fife KY1 2SB
Tel: 01592 643777
www.forbo-flooring.co.uk
Britain's only linoleum
maker with 30 colours in
domestic range and over 60
in the contract selection.

Formica
Coast Road, North Shields
Tyne & Wear NE29 8RE
Tel: 0191 2593000; for
samples tel 0191 2593512
www.formica-europe.com
Over 550 colours for
worktops and surfaces.

Francesca's Lime Wash
34 Battersea
Business Centre
99–109 Lavender Hill
London SW11 5QL
Tel: 020 7228 7694
www.francescaspaint.com
Traditional lime wash.
Colour matching and
custom colour mixing.

Anna French
36 Hinton Road
London SE24 0HJ
Tel: 020 7737 6555
www.annafrench.co.uk
Fabrics, lace, voiles, sheers,
wallpapers and accessories.
Designs for children.

Pierre Frey UK Ltd
251–253 Fulham Road
London SW3 6HY
Tel: 020 7376 5599
www.pierrefrey.com
Vast range of stylish printed
fabrics and textured plains.

C H Frost
67 Abingdon Road
London W8 6AN
Tel: 020 7937 0451
Reupholstery, loose covers,
curtains and blinds.

**The Gallery of Antique
Costume and Textiles**
2 Church Street
London NW8 8ED
Tel: 020 7723 9981
www.gact.co.uk
Antique textiles and
tapestries.

Gilt Edge Carpets
255 New King's Road
London SW6 4RB
Tel: 020 7731 2588
www.giltedgecarpets.co.uk
Carpets and natural/
hardwood flooring.

Grand Illusions
P.O. Box 81
Shaftesbury
Dorset SP7 8TA
Tel: 01747 858300
www.grandillusions.co.uk
Furniture inspired by French
country style.

Judy Greenwood Antiques
657–659 Fulham Road
London SW6 5PY
Tel: 020 7736 6037
Textiles, notably quilts –
English, Welsh, French,
American and Canadian.
French monogrammed
linen and hemp sheets
and French curtains.

Habitat
196–199 Tottenham Court
Road
London W1T 9PJ
Tel: 08444 991122, ring
08444 991111 for branches
www.habitat.net
Paints, fabrics and
accessories are good value
and up-to-the-minute.

Hamilton-Weston Wallpapers
Marryat Courtyard
88 Sheen Road
Richmond, Surrey TW9 1UF
Tel: 020 8940 4850
www.hamiltonweston.com
Archive wallpaper and
hand-blockprinted papers.

Hammerite Products Ltd
Customer Care Centre
Wexham Road
Slough
Berkshire SL2 5DS
Telephone: 0870 4441111
www.hammerite.com
Paints for metal in huge
range and three finishes
(smooth, hammered, satin).

L G Harris & Co
Stoke Prior
Bromsgrove
Worcestershire B60 4AE
Tel: 01527 575441
Good quality brushes and
decorating tools.

Nicholas Haslam
12–14 Holbein Place
London SW1W 8NL
Tel: 020 7730 8623
www.nicholashaslam.com
Custom-made painted
furniture plus lights,
fabrics and upholstery.

Heal's
196 Tottenham Court Road
London W1T 7LQ
Tel: 020 7636 1666
www.heals.co.uk
Famous modernist store has
bed and table linen,
furnishing fabrics, curtain
and blind-making service.

Nicholas Herbert Ltd
118 Lots Road
London SW10 0RJ
Tel: 020 7376 5596
www.nicholasherbert.com
Fabric printed with
18th- and 19th-century
French designs.

**James Hetley Stained Glass
Supplies Ltd**
Glasshouse Fields
London E1 9JA
Tel: 020 7780 2344
www.hetleys.co.uk
Coloured, stained and
etched glass, leaded
windows.

The Holding Company
241–245 Kings Road
London SW3 5EL
Tel: 020 7352 1600 or
020 8445 2888 (warehouse
shop).
www.theholding
company.co.uk
Storage for every room,
plus accessories.

Howe
93 Pimlico Road
London SW1W 8PH
Tel: 020 7730 7987
www.howelondon.com
Wide variety of natural
hand-dyed Moroccan grain
goat skins and Italian hides
and suedes: different colours
and textures; printed skins.

Ikea
Brent Park
2 Drury Way
North Circular Road
London NW10 OTH
Tel: 0845 3551141
www.ikea.com
Inexpensive fabrics, bed
linen and accessories.

The Isle Mill
Tower House
Ruthvenfield Road
Inveralmond
Perth PH1 3UN
Tel: 01738 609090
www.isle.mill.com
Wool tartans and plaids,
many designs of furnishing
silks, special design projects.

Jen Jones
Pontbrendu
Llanybydder
Ceredigion
Wales SA40 9UJ
Tel: 01570 480610
www.jen-jones.com
Designer, cottage and
collectors' quilts, as well as
blankets and old linen.

Junckers
Unit A, 1 Wheaton Road
Witham
Essex CM8 3UJ
Tel: 01376 534700
www.junckers.com
Hardwood worktops in
range of timbers.

Kirkstone Quarries
Skelwith Bridge
Ambleside
Cumbria LA22 9NN
Tel: 01539 433296
www.kirkstone.com
Limestone, slate, granite,
mosaic and glass flooring,
worktops and surfaces.

Lelièvre UK
Chelsea Harbour Design
Centre
London SW10 0XE
Tel: 020 7352 4798
www.lelievre.co.uk
Top of the range fabrics.

John Lewis
Oxford Street
London W1A 1EX
Tel: 020 7629 7711
www.johnlewis.com
Excellent value and huge
range of bed linen, fabrics
and trimmings.

Lewis & Wood
Woodchester Mill
North Woodchester, Stroud
Gloucestershire GL5 5NN
Tel: 01453 878517
www.lewisandwood.co.uk
Wallpapers including
hunting, shooting and
fishing designs, stripes,
tartan, *toile de Jouy*.
Heavyweight plain linens for
curtains and upholstery.

Liberty
214–220 Regent Street
London W1R 6AH
Tel: 020 7734 1234
www.liberty.co.uk
Eclectic collection of fabrics.

Malabar
31–33 South Bank
Business Centre
Ponton Road
London SW8 5BL
Tel: 020 7501 4200
www.malabar.co.uk
Handloomed cotton plains,
stripes and checks, jute, wild
silk, wool and crewel work
inspired by Indian designs.

Ian Mankin
109 Regents Park Road
London NW1 8UR
Tel: 020 7722 0997
www.ianmankinonline.
co.uk
Noted for his tickings,
ginghams, muslins and
plains in heavy cotton.

Andrew Martin
200 Walton Street
London SW3 2JL
Tel: 020 7225 5100
www.andrewmartin.co.uk
Textural fabrics in raffia,
velvet and faux suede,
plus furniture.

Melin Tregwynt
Tregwynt Mill, Castlemorris
Haverfordwest
Pembrokeshire SA62 5UX
Tel: 01348 891225
Mail order: 01348 891644
www.melintregwynt.co.uk
Woollen blankets, throws,
bedspreads and cushions
woven in Welsh mill.

Andrew Muirhead & Son Ltd
Dalmarnock Leather Works
273–289 Dunn Street
Glasgow G40 3EA
Tel: 0141 5543724
www.muirhead.co.uk
Leather for wall panelling,
desks – even aircraft.

Muji
41 Carnaby Street
London W1V 1PD
and other stores
throughout London
and the UK
Tel: 020 7287 7323
www.mujionline.com
Minimalist accessories
from Japan.

Ray Munn
861–863 Fulham Road
London SW6 5HP
Tel: 020 7736 9876
www.raymunn.com
Swedish eco-friendly paints
that can be colour matched.

**Natural Building
Technologies Ltd**
The Hangar,
Worminghall Road, Oakley
Bucks HP18 9UL
Tel: 01844 338338
www.natural-building.co.uk
Decorating materials, earth
products, lime products,
insulation materials and
timber. Eco-friendly paints.

The Natural Fabric Company
Dovedale Farmhouse
Blockley, Moreton-in-Marsh,
Gloucestershire GL56 9TS
Tel: 01386 700900
www.naturalfabric
company.com
Calico, jute, hessian and
other natural fabrics.

Nutshell Natural Paints
Unit 3, Leigham Units
Silverton Road
Matford Park
Exeter
Devon EX2 8HY
Tel: 01392 823760
www.nutshellpaints.com
Casein milk paints, floor
paint, colourwashes, all
eco-friendly.

Oka
Tel: 0844 8157380
www.okadirect.com
By mail order, stylish china,
furniture and accessories,
most sourced in Far East.

Options Marble
Unit 37A Grace
Business Centre
23 Willow Lane
Mitcham
Surrey CR4 4TU
Tel: 020 8640 3560
Marble worktops and
surfaces, stone floors,
hearths and fire surrounds.

Osborne & Little
304 King's Road
London SW3 5UH
Tel: 020 7352 1456
www.osborneandlittle.com
Regular collections of new
fabrics and wallpapers.

The Paint Library
5 Elystan Street
London SW3 3NT
Tel: 020 7823 7755
www.paintlibrary.co.uk
Paints by David Oliver and
Nina Campbell, papers from
David Oliver, Neisha Crosland
and Emily Todhunter.

Paper Moon
The Studio
3 Hill Road
London NW8 9QE
Tel: 020 7286 9455
www.papermoon.co.uk
A vast range of fabrics
and wallpapers including
sky wallpaper.

Papers and Paints
4 Park Walk
London SW10 0AD
Tel: 020 7352 8626
www.papers–paints.co.uk
One of the widest ranges
of paint colours, they can
also colour match samples.
Advice on choosing colours.
Consultancy on decoration
of historical buildings.

Photo-Furnishings
The Studio
116b Highlever Road
London W10 6PL
Tel: 020 8960 1102
www.photo-furnishings.com
Photo-printed wallpapers
and textiles.

Simon Playle
6 Fulham Park Studios
London SW6 4LW
Tel: 020 7371 0131
Fine Swiss and fire-retardant
voiles, handprinted papers
and Brussels Weave carpets
in custom colours.

Pongees
28–30 Hoxton Square
London N1 6NN
Tel: 020 7739 9130
www.pongees.com
Over 100 different qualities
of silk, both plain dyed and
jacquards.

Potmolen Paints
27 Woodcock
Industrial Estate
Warminster
Wiltshire BA12 9DX
Tel: 01985 213960
Historic paints, limewashes
and linseed oil paints.

Prêt à Vivre
The Curtain Room
Shelton Lodge, Shelton
Newark, Notts NG23 5JJ
Tel: 0845 1305161
www.pretavivre.com
Curtains, fabric blinds,
wooden and aluminium
venetian blinds (wooden
blinds can be painted in
Farrow & Ball or Dulux
colours), quilts.

Lena Proudlock
4 The Chipping
Tetbury
Gloucestershire GL8 8ET
Tel: 01666 500051
www.lenaproudlock.com
Fabrics – furnishing denim
in over 50 colours – and
accessories.

Purves & Purves
Tel: 020 8893 4000 (online
shopping) and 020 8898
2318 (interior design
service)
www.purves.co.uk
Contemporary furniture,
lighting and household
accessories.

Relics of Witney
Unit 12, Crawley Mill
Industrial Estate
Dry Lane
Witney
Oxon OX29 9TJ
Tel: 01993 704611
www.tryrelics.co.uk
Paints and wallpapers
including heritage ranges,
Liberon waxes, brushes for
complex decorating.

Rose of Jericho
Horchester Farm
Holywell, nr. Evershot
Dorchester DT2 0LL
Tel: 01935 83676
www.rose-of-jericho.
    demon.co.uk
Historic paints and mortars.

Russell & Chapple
68 Drury Lane
London WC2B 5SP
Tel: 020 7836 7521
www.russellandchapple.
    co.uk
Canvas, jute, muslin
and hessian.

Jane Sacchi Linens Ltd
Tel: 020 7351 3160
www.janesacchi.com
Antique and reproduction
textiles based on French
linens. Furnishing fabrics,
hemp and vegetable-dyed
bed linens

Sanderson
See website for stockists
www.sanderson–uk.com
Morris range of historical
paint colours available in
eggshell and vinyl matt
emulsion, furnishing fabrics,
upholstered furniture.

Sandtex
See website for stockists
www.sandtex.co.uk
Exterior paints and
renderings.

**Sinclair Till Flooring
Company**
791–793 Wandsworth Road
London SW8 3JQ
Tel: 020 7720 0031
www.sinclairtill.co.uk
Floor coverings – lino, vinyl,
rubber and cork.

Sixty 6
66 Marylebone High Street
London W1M 3AH
Tel: 020 7224 6066
Vintage furniture, clothing
and accessories.

**Annie Sloan's Traditional
Paint Range**
117 London Road
Oxford, OX3 9HZ UK
Tel: 01865 768666
www.anniesloan.com
Paints, brushes, stencils,
découpage, gilding
supplies, home decorating
books, varnish, glaze,
blanks, pigment, grainers.
Courses in painting and
decorative techniques.

Soane
50 Pimlico Road
London SW1W 8LP
Tel: 020 7730 6400
www.soane.co.uk
Floor coverings, antique
replicas.

George Spencer
33 Elystan Street
London, SW3 3NT
Tel: 020 7584 3003
www.georgespencer.com
Contemporary fabrics.

Spina
12 Kingsgate Place
London NW6 4TA
Tel: 020 7328 5274
www.spinadesign.co.uk
Tie-backs, tassels, cushions.

Stencil Bazaar
The Old Village Paint Store
Heart of the Country Village
London Road
Swinfen, Lichfield
Staffs WS14 9QR
Tel: 01543 480669
Historic paints and stencils.

Tarkett Sommer Ltd
Century House
Bridgwater Road
Worcester WR4 9FA
Tel: 01905 342700
Lino and vinyls for floors,
also wood flooring.

Tempus Stet
1 Button Farm
Brentwood Road
Brentwood
Essex CM13 3PN
Tel: 01277 810995
www.tempus–stet.com
Tables, chairs, headboards,
lamps, mirrors, pelmets,
curtain tie-backs and finials
in antique styles.

Tidmarsh & Sons
Unit 14, Ash Industrial
Estate
Flex Meadow
Harlow, Essex CM19 5TJ
Tel: 01279 401960
www.tidmarsh.co.uk
Blinds in customers' fabrics,
made to measure for
awkward windows,
woodslat blinds in big
range of colours.

Timney Fowler
Unit 2 Avondale
Industrial Estate
Avondale Road
Edgeley, Stockport
Cheshire SK3 0UD
Tel: 0161 477 4225
www.timneyfowler.org.uk
Furnishing fabrics using
classical and old prints in
modern context.

Toast
D Ashmount Park
Upper Forest Way
Llansamlet
Swansea SA6 8QR
Tel: 0844 5575200
www.toast.co.uk
Bed linen, cushions,
blankets and throws, rugs
and mats, and household
accessories.

Tobias and the Angel
68 White Hart Lane
London SW13 0PZ
Tel: 020 8878 8902
www.tobiasandtheangel.
com
Painted furniture with a
Scandinavian feel, fabrics,
old-fashioned, antiqued
and rustic accessories. Also
interior design service.

UK Hide Company
Unit 11 Trade City
Avro Way
Brooklands
Weybridge KT13 0XQ
Tel: 01932 353338
www.ukhide.co.uk
Supplier of Connolly hides.

V V Rouleaux
54 Sloane Square
London SW1W 8AX
Tel: 020 7730 3125
www.vvrouleaux.com
Exciting ribbons and trims.

V'soske Joyce (UK)
16 Coda Centre
189 Munster Road
London SW6 6AW
Tel: 020 7386 7200
Dyed-to-match carpets, art
rugs/wallhangings.

Pierre Vuillemenot Ltd
42 Woodfield Avenue
London SW16 1LG
Tel/fax: 020 8769 9292
Fabric walling specialist
and curtain maker.

Sasha Waddell
Tel: 020 8979 9189
www.sashawaddell.co.uk
Painted furniture in the
Swedish style.

**Watts of Westminster
incorporating Belinda
Coote Tapestries**
3/14 Chelsea Harbour
Design Centre
London SW10 0XE
Tel: 020 7376 4486
www.wattsof
westminster.co.uk
Traditional tapestry and
jacquard weave fabrics,
trimmings and wallpapers.

The White Company
Stores throughout the UK
Tel: 0845 6788150
www.thewhitecompany.
com
Bed linen, towels.

Joanna Wood
48a Pimlico Road
London SW1W 8LP
Tel: 020 7730 5064
www.joannawood.co.uk
Home products including
table linen, cushions,
throws and tableware.

Yarwood Leather
Treefield Industrial Estate
Gelderd Road
Morley
Leeds LS27 7JU
Tel: 0113 2521014
www.yarwood.co.uk
Upholstery leather and
bespoke service.

Zoffany
Chalfont House
Oxford Road
Denham
Buckinghamshire UB9 4DX
Tel: 08708 300350
www.zoffany.com
Stockists throughout
the UK
Historic paints and
wallpaper including
National Trust collection.

picture credits

Key: **ph**=photographer, **a**=above, **b**=below, **c**=centre, **l**=left, **r**=right

1 ph Alan Williams/private apartment in London designed by Hugh Broughton Architects; **2 ph** James Merrell/Consuelo Zoelly's apartment in Paris; **3l ph** Simon Upton; **3r ph** Alan Williams/Warner Johnson's apartment in New York designed by Edward Cabot of Cabot Design Ltd; **4–5 ph** Alan Williams/Alannah Weston's house in London designed by Stickland Coombe Architecture; **6l ph** Alan Williams/Warner Johnson's apartment in New York designed by Edward Cabot of Cabot Design Ltd; **6r ph** Alan Williams/an apartment in Paris designed by Géraldine Prieur, an interior designer fascinated with colour; **7l ph** James Merrell/Gabriele Sanders's apartment in New York; **7r ph** Chris Everard/interior designer Ann Boyd's own apartment in London; **8 ph** Tom Leighton; **9ac ph** Tomas Stewart; **9ar ph** Henry Bourne; **9c ph** Alan Williams; **9cr ph** Polly Wreford/Clare Nash's house in London; **9bl ph** James Merrell; **11 ph** Alan Williams/Lindsay Taylor's apartment in Glasgow; **12al ph** Simon Upton; **12bl ph** Alan Williams/
Toia Saibene's apartment in Milan; **12r ph** James Merrell; **13a ph** Christopher Drake/Ali Sharland's house in Gloucestershire; **13bl ph** Alan Williams/Lisa Fine's apartment in Paris; **13br ph** Alan Williams/the Arbuthnott family's house near Cirencester designed by Nicholas Arbuthnott, fabrics designed by Vanessa Arbuthnott; **14al ph** Alan Williams/Warner Johnson's apartment in New York designed by Edward Cabot of Cabot Design Ltd; **14ar ph** Andrew Wood/Nanna Ditzel's home in Copenhagen; **14b ph** Chris Everard/Philippe Model's apartment in Paris; **15l ph** Alan Williams/Gail and Barry Stephens's house in London; **15r ph** Polly Wreford/Marie-Hélène de Taillac's pied-à-terre in Paris; **16l ph** Alan Williams/interior designer Roberto Bergero's own apartment in Paris; **16r ph** Ray Main/Julie Prisca's house in Normandy; **17l ph** Alan Williams/Donata Sartorio's apartment in Milan; **17ar ph** Alan Williams/Warner Johnson's apartment in New York designed by Edward Cabot of Cabot Design Ltd; **17b ph** Tom Leighton; **18l ph** Alan Williams/private apartment in London designed by Hugh Broughton Architects; **18r ph** Alan Williams/owner of Gloss, Pascale Bredillet's own apartment in London; **19** © The Color Wheel Company (www.colorwheelco.com t. +1 541 929 7526); **20 ph** Andrew Wood/Neil Bingham's house in Blackheath, London; **21a both ph** James Merrell/Sally Butler's house in London; **21b both ph** Alan Williams/Richard Oyarzarbal's apartment in London designed by Urban Research Laboratory; **22 ph** Alan Willams the Arbuthnott family's house near Cirencester designed by Nicholas Arbuthnott, fabrics designed by Vanessa Arbuthnott; **23l ph** Alan Williams/interior designer and Managing Director of the Société Yves Halard, Michelle Halard's own apartment in Paris; **23ar ph** James Merrell; **23br ph** Alan Williams/Alannah Weston's house in London designed by Stickland Coombe Architecture; **24al ph** Alan Williams/Gail and Barry Stephens's house in London; **24ar ph** Alan Williams/Donata Sartorio's apartment in Milan; **24b ph** Alan Williams/an apartment in Paris designed by Géraldine Prieur, an interior designer fascinated with colour; **25al** Andrew Wallace's house in London; **25ar ph** Andrew Wood/Mary Shaw's Sequana apartment in Paris; **25b ph** Alan Williams/Lisa Fine's apartment in Paris; **26 ph** Chris Everard/Eric de Queker's apartment in Antwerp; **27a both ph** Alan Williams/the architect Voon Wong's own apartment in London; **27b ph** Alan Williams/Director of design consultants Graven Images, Janice Kirkpatrick's apartment in Glasgow; **28a ph** Alan Williams/Lindsay Taylor's apartment in Glasgow; **28bl ph** Simon Upton; **28br ph** Christopher Drake/Juan Corbella's apartment in London designed by HM2, Richard Webb with Andrew Hanson; **29a ph** Alan Williams/architect Eric Liftin's own apartment in New York; **29b ph** Alan Williams/Director of design consultants Graven Images, Janice Kirkpatrick's apartment in Glasgow; **30a ph** Catherine Gratwicke/artist Hunt Slonem's own loft in New York; **31b ph** James Merrell/Milly de Cabrol's apartment in New York; **31a ph** Christopher Drake/Marisa Cavalli's home in Milan; **31bl ph** Alan Williams/Donata Sartorio's apartment in Milan; **31br ph** Alan Willams/the Arbuthnott family's house near Cirencester designed by Nicholas Arbuthnott, fabrics designed by Vanessa Arbuthnott; **32al ph** Polly Wreford/Marie-Hélène de Taillac's pied-à-terre in Paris; **32r ph** Polly Wreford/Lena Proudlock's house in Gloucestershire; **32bl ph** Chris Everard/Mark Weinstein's apartment in New York designed by Lloyd Schwan; **33a ph** Alan Williams/interior designer John Barman's own apartment in New York; **33bl ph** Alan Williams/Richard Oyarzarbal's apartment in London designed by Urban Research Laboratory; **33br ph** Polly Wreford; **34 ph** Tom Leighton; **35al ph** Christopher Drake; **35ac ph**

James Merrell; **35ar ph** Jan Baldwin/a house in Cape Elizabeth designed by Stephen Blatt Architects; **35bl ph** Alan Williams; **35c ph** Tom Leighton/paint Farrow & Ball: floor Mouse's Back floor paint no. 40, cupboards Green Smoke no. 47 and interior Red Fox no. 48, walls and woodwork String no. 8, ceiling Off White no. 3; **35br ph** Alan Williams/Alannah Weston's house in London designed by Stickland Coombe Architecture; **36a ph** Henry Bourne; **36l ph** Alan Williams/an apartment in Paris designed by Géraldine Prieur, an interior designer fascinated with colour; **36bc ph** Polly Wreford; **36br ph** Henry Bourne; **37a ph** Tom Leighton; **37b both ph** Alan Williams/the architect Voon Wong's own apartment in London; **38a ph** Henry Bourne; **38bl ph** Christopher Drake/refurbishment and interior design by Chicchi Meroni Fassio, Parnassus; **38br ph** Christopher Drake/designer Barbara Davis's own house in upstate New York; **39al ph** Alan Williams/interior designer Roberto Bergero's own apartment in Paris; **39ar&b ph** Christopher Drake/designer Barbara Davis's own house in upstate New York; **40a ph** Polly Wreford/Lena Proudlock's house in Gloucestershire; **40b ph** Polly Wreford/Liz Stirling's apartment in Paris; **41al ph** Christopher Drake/designed by Lorraine Kirke; **41ar ph** Polly Wreford/Daniel Jasiak's apartment in Paris; **41bl ph** Alan Williams/Katie Bassford King's house in London designed by Touch Interior Design; **41br ph** David Montgomery/Sheila Scholes's house near Cambridge; **42a ph** Henry Bourne; **42bl ph** Alan Williams/Lindsay Taylor's apartment in Glasgow; **42br ph** Alan Williams/Director of design consultants Graven Images, Janice Kirkpatrick's apartment in Glasgow; **43a ph** Simon Upton; **43c ph** Alan Williams/Warner Johnson's apartment in New York designed by Edward Cabot of Cabot Design Ltd; **43b ph** Alan Williams/Miv Watts's house in Norfolk; **44 both ph** Alan Williams/interior designer and Managing Director of the Société Yves Halard, Michelle Halard's own apartment in Paris; **45a both ph** Alan Williams/an apartment in Paris designed by Géraldine Prieur, an interior designer fascinated with colour; **45b both ph** Alan Williams/Marilea and Guido Somarè's apartment in Milan; **46 ph** Tom Leighton; **47ac ph** Tom Leighton; **47ar ph** Martin Brigdale; **47c & 47bl ph** James Merrell; **47br ph** James Merrell; **48 ph** James Merrell/Janie Jackson, stylist and designer; **50a ph** Tom Leighton; **50b ph** Andrew Wood/Gabriele Sanders's apartment in New York; **51al ph** Chris Everard/Signora Venturini's apartment in Milan; **51ar ph** Andrew Wood/Johanne Riss's house in Brussels; **51b ph** Andrew Wood/Jane Collins of Sixty 6 in Marylebone High Street, home in central London; **52 all ph** Simon Upton; **53al ph** Andrew Wood/Johanne Riss's house in Brussels; **53ar ph** Andrew Wood/Paul and Carolyn Morgan's house in Wales; **53b ph** Tom Leighton/all linens The White Company; armoire and chair Josephine Ryan; **54a ph** Polly Wreford/The Sawmills Studio; **54b ph** Henry Bourne; **55 al ph** Chris Everard/an apartment in London designed by Jo Hagan of USE Architects; **55ar ph** Chris Everard/the Sugarman-Behun house on Long Island; **55b ph** Simon Upton; **56 & 57b ph** Jan Baldwin/Laurence and Yves Sabourets's house in Brittany; **57a ph** Simon Upton; **58a ph** Polly Wreford; **58l ph** Chris Everard/an apartment in Milan designed by Daniela Micol Wajskol, interior designer, chairs from Cristina Bellini Antiquario, Milan; **58r ph** Polly Wreford/Sheila Scholes and Gunter Schmidt's house in Cambridgeshire; **59al ph** Chris Everard/an apartment in Milan designed by Daniela Micol Wajskol, interior designer, picture above mantelpiece from L'oro dei Farlocchi, Milan; **59ar ph** Tom Leighton; **59b ph** Chris Everard/an apartment in Milan designed by Daniela Micol Wajskol, interior designer, Chinese rug from Alberto Levy Gallery, Milan, round table and screen from L'oro dei Farlocchi, Milan, bronze lamp from Polenghi e Maffei Antiquari, Milan; **60l ph** Tom Leighton/Roger and Fay Oates's house in Herefordshire (The Long Barn, Eastnor, Ledbury, Herefordshire HR8 1EL, t. 01531 632718); **60r ph** Henry Bourne; **61a ph** Christopher Drake/Eva Johnson's house in Suffolk, interiors designed by Eva Johnson; **61bl ph** Chris Everard/Suzanne Slesin and Michael Steinberg's apartment in New York – design by Jean-Louis Ménard; **61br ph** Chris Everard/Eric de Queker's apartment in Antwerp; **62al ph** Alan Williams/Gail and Barry Stephens's house in London; **62ar ph** Tom Leighton/Keith Varty and Alan Cleaver's apartment in London designed by Jonathan Reed/Reed Boyd (t. 020 7565 0066); **62b ph** Andrew Wood/Chelsea loft apartment in New York, designed by The Moderns; **63 ph** Andrew Wood/Norma Holland's house in London; **64a ph** Alan Williams; **64b ph** Andrew Wood/the Caroline Deforest House in Pasadena, California, home of Michael Murray and Kelly Jones; **65a ph** Andrew Wood/Curtice Booth's house in Pasadena, California; **65b ph** Andrew Wood/the King House in Mammoth Lakes, California; **66a&c ph** Tom Leighton; **66b ph** James Merrell; **67a**

ph Alan Williams/Stanley and Nancy Grossman's apartment in New York designed by Jennifer Post Design; **67b both ph** Alan Williams/Katie Bassford King's house in London designed by Touch Interior Design; **68l ph** Alan Williams/Alannah Weston's house in London designed by Stickland Coombe Architecture; **68r both ph** Alan Williams/Katie Bassford King's house in London designed by Touch Interior Design; **69l ph** Tom Leighton/a house in London designed by Charles Rutherfoord, 51 The Chase, London SW4 0NP (t. 020 7627 0182); **69ar ph** Andrew Wood/Jamie Falla and Lynn Graham's house in London; **69br ph** Polly Wreford/an apartment in New York designed by Belmont Freeman Architects; **70a ph** Pia Tryde; **70bl ph** Alan Williams/Warner Johnson's apartment in New York designed by Edward Cabot of Cabot Design Ltd; **70br ph** Alan Williams/Lindsay Taylor's apartment in Glasgow; **71a ph** Chris Everard/an apartment in New York designed by Gabellini Associates; **71bl&bc ph** Chris Everard/Eric de Queker's apartment in Antwerp; **71br ph** Chris Everard/Gomez-Murphy loft, Hoxton, London designed by Urban Salon Ltd; **72 both ph** Alan Williams/Stanley and Nancy Grossman's apartment in New York designed by Jennifer Post Design; **73a both ph** Andrew Wood/Chelsea studio New York City, designed by Marino + Giolito; **73b ph** Thomas Stewart/Yuen-Wei Chew's apartment in London designed by Paul Daly represented by Echo Design Agency; **74a ph** Chris Everard/an apartment in Milan designed by Daniela Micol Wajskol, interior designer, kitchen table and chairs from Polenghi Antiquario, Milan; **74b ph** Chris Everard/John Minshaw's house in London designed by John Minshaw; **75al ph** Henry Bourne; **75ar ph** Andrew Wood/The Glendale, California, home of John and Heather Banfield; **75bl&bc ph** Henry Bourne; **75br ph** Alan Williams; **76 ph** Tom Leighton; **77ac ph** Polly Wreford; **77ar ph** Catherine Gratwicke/Agnès Emery's house in Brussels, tiles from Emery & Cie; **77c&cr ph** Tom Leighton; **77bl ph** Jan Baldwin; **77br ph** Catherine Gratwicke; **79 ph** Alan Williams/Alannah Weston's house in London designed by Stickland Coombe Architecture; **80a ph** Pia Tryde; **80b ph** David Montgomery/a house in Connecticut designed by Lynn Morgan Design; **81al ph** Christopher Drake/designer Barbara Davis's own house in upstate New York; **81ar ph** Christopher Drake/designed by Lorraine Kirke; **81b ph** Simon Upton/Lena Proudlock's house in Gloucestershire; **82 ph** Alan Williams/Alannah Weston's house in London designed by Stickland Coombe Architecture; **83al ph** Andrew Wood/Alastair Hendy and John Clinch's apartment in London designed by Alastair Hendy; **83ar ph** Alan Williams/Richard Oyarzabal's apartment in London designed by Urban Research Laboratory; **83bl ph** Polly Wreford/Lena Proudlock's house in Gloucestershire; **83br ph** Andrew Wood/Kurt Bredenbeck's apartment at the Barbican, London; **84a ph** Simon Upton; **84b ph** Henry Bourne/Dan and Claire Thorne's townhouse designed by Sarah Featherstone of Hudson Featherstone; **85 all ph** Alan Williams/Richard Oyarzabal's apartment in London designed by Urban Research Laboratory; **86l ph** Christopher Drake/Enrica Stabile's house in Brunello; **86ar ph** Alan Williams/Marilea and Guido Somarè's apartment in Milan; **86br & 87a ph** Chris Tubbs/Daniel Jasiak's home near Biarritz; **87b ph** Simon Upton/Lena Proudlock's house in Gloucestershire; **88a ph** Chris Tubbs; **88b ph** Alan Williams/Miv Watts's house in Norfolk; **89al ph** Tom Leighton; **89ar ph** Alan Williams/Donata Sartorio's apartment in Milan; **89br ph** Tom Leighton; **90 ph** Andrew Wood/Anthony and Julia Collett's house in London designed by Anthony Collett of Collett Zarzycki Ltd; **91al ph** James Merrell; **91ar ph** Fritz von der Schulenburg/a house in Pennsylvania designed by Laura Bohn of L.B.D.A.; **91b ph** Alan Williams/interior designer and Managing Director of the Société Yves Halard, Michelle Halard's own apartment in Paris; **92a ph** Simon Upton; **92bl ph** Chris Everard/an apartment in Milan designed by Nicoletta Marazza; **92br & 93r ph** Jan Baldwin/Elena Colombo's cottage on the east end of Long Island; **93l ph** Catherine Gratwicke/Agnès Emery's house in Brussels; **94a ph** Alan Williams/Hudson Street loft in New York designed by Moneo Brock Studio; **94b ph** Alan Williams/the architect Voon Wong's own apartment in London; **95al ph** Henry Bourne; **95ac ph** Simon Upton; **95ar ph** Tom Leighton; **95bl ph** James Merrell; **95bc ph** Tham Nhu-Tran; **95br ph** Alan Williams; **96a ph** Pia Tryde; **96bl ph** Alan Williams/Donata Sartorio's apartment in Milan; **96br ph** Andrew Wood/Mary Shaw's Sequana apartment in Paris; **97al ph** Alan Williams/Warner Johnson's apartment in New York designed by Edward Cabot of Cabot Design Ltd; **97ar ph** James Merrell; **97b ph** Christopher Drake/Enrica Stabile's house in Brunello; **98 all ph** James Merrell/Sally Butler's house in London; **99l ph** Debi Treloar/Ab Rogers and Sophie Braimbridge's house, London, designed by Richard Rogers for his mother. Furniture design by

KRD–Kitchen Rogers Design; **99r ph** Debi Treloar/Vincent and Frieda Plasschaert's house in Brugge, Belgium; **100–101 ph** Christopher Drake/Juan Corbella's apartment in London designed by HM2, Richard Webb with Andrew Hanson; **102a ph** Simon Upton; **102b ph** Pia Tryde; **103al ph** Fritz von der Schulenburg/Irene and Giorgio Silvagni's house in Provence; **103ar&b ph** Simon Upton; **104l ph** Tom Leighton; **104r ph** Andrew Wood/Kurt Bredenbeck's apartment at the Barbican, London; **105al ph** James Merrell/an apartment in Paris designed by Hervé Vermesch; **105ar ph** James Merrell/Vicky and Simon Young's house in Northumberland; **105b ph** Ray Main/John Howell's loft in London designed by Circus Architects; **106a ph** Andrew Wood/an apartment in London designed by Littman Goddard Hogarth; **106b ph** Andrew Wood/an apartment in the San Remo on the Upper West Side of Manhattan, designed by John L. Stewart and Michael D'Arcy of SIT; **107 ph** Andrew Wood/an apartment in London designed by Littman Goddard Hogarth; **108a ph** Peter Cassidy; **108b ph** Chris Everard/an apartment in Milan designed by Nicoletta Marazza; **109l ph** Simon Upton; **109ar ph** Alan Williams/Maria Jesus Polanco's apartment in New York designed by Hut Sachs Studio in collaboration with Moneo Brock Studio; **109br ph** Alan Williams/Lisa Fine's apartment in Paris; **110 ph** Henry Bourne/Linda Trahair's house in Bath; **111l ph** Chris Everard/a house in Paris designed by Bruno Tanquerel; **111r both ph** Simon Upton; **112a ph** Simon Upton; **112b ph** Chris Everard/Karen Davies's apartment in London designed by Joëlle Darby; **113al&ac ph** Henry Bourne; **113ar ph** Tom Leighton; **113bl ph** Alan Williams/Lisa Fine's apartment in Paris; **113bc ph** Andrew Wood; **113br ph** Thomas Stewart; **114a ph** Christopher Drake; **114b ph** Tom Leighton/Sally Butler's house in London; **115a** Chris Everard/an apartment in Milan designed by Nicoletta Marazza; **115b ph** Alan Williams/owner of Gloss, Pascale Bredillet's own apartment in London; **116a&br ph** Tom Leighton; **116bl ph** James Merrell; **117 ph** Alan Williams/New York apartment designed by Bruce Bierman; **118 ph** Fritz von der Schulenburg/Irene and Giorgio Silvagni's house in Provence; **119l ph** Catherine Gratwicke/antique mirrored bedthrow from the Gallery of Antique Costumes and Textiles, striped throw from Selfridges; **119r ph** Alan Williams/interior designer and Managing Director of the Société Yves Halard, Michelle Halard's own apartment in Paris; **120 all ph** Alan Williams/interior designer John Barman's own apartment in New York; **121 ph** Christopher Drake/Juan Corbella's apartment in London designed by HM2, Richard Webb with Andrew Hanson; **122a ph** Tom Leighton; **122cl,bl&r ph** Alan Williams/an apartment in Paris designed by Géraldine Prieur, an interior designer fascinated with colour; **123 ph** Polly Wreford/Liz Stirling's apartment in Paris; **124 ph** Chris Everard/the London apartment of the Sheppard Day Design Partnership; **125 ph** James Merrell/ Sophie Sarin's flat in London; **126l ph** Polly Wreford/Louise Jackson's house in London; **126r ph** Fritz von der Schulenburg/Piero Castellini Baldissera's house in Montalcino, Siena; **127 ph** David Montgomery/Laura Bohn's apartment in New York designed by Laura Bohn Design Associates; **128 ph** Alan Williams/interior designer and Managing Director of the Société Yves Halard, Michelle Halard's own apartment in Paris; **129a ph** Alan Williams; **129c&b ph** Alan Williams/interior designer and Managing Director of the Société Yves Halard, Michelle Halard's own apartment in Paris; **130l ph** Tom Leighton; **130r ph** James Merrell; **131 ph** Alan Williams/Selworthy apartment in London designed by Gordana Mandic and Peter Tyler at Buildburo (www.buildburo.co.uk); **132a ph** Tom Leighton; **132b ph** Alan Williams/Richard Oyarzabal's apartment in London designed by Urban Research Laboratory; **133l ph** Alan Williams; **133ac ph** Tom Leighton; **133ar ph** Thomas Stewart; **133bl ph** Polly Wreford; **133bc ph** James Merrell; **133br ph** Tom Leighton; **134 ph** Tom Leighton; **135al ph** Tom Leighton; **135ac ph** Henry Bourne; **135c ph** Simon Upton; **135cr ph** Henry Bourne; **135bl&br ph** Tom Leighton; **137 ph** Alan Williams/ the Arbuthnott family's house near Cirencester designed by Nicholas Arbuthnott, fabrics designed by Vanessa Arbuthnott; **160 ph** Alan Williams/the architect Voon Wong's own apartment in London.

In addition to the designers and home owners mentioned above, the publisher would like to thank the following: Elie Mouyal, Mimmi O'Connell, Marilyn Phipps, Liz Dougherty Pierce, José de Yturbe, Tricia Foley, Dot Spikings and Jennifer Castle, Katie Fontana and Tony Niblock, Bill Blass, Jan Moereels, Jo Crepain, Jon Geir and Inger Høyersten, and Mary Drysdale.

architects and designers whose work has been featured in this book:

Key: *a*=above, *b*=below,
c=centre, *l*=left, *r*=right

Nicholas Arbuthnott
Arbuthnott Ladenbury Architects
Architects and urban designers
15 Gosditch Street
Cirencester GL7 2AG
and
Vanessa Arbuthnott Fabrics
The Tallet
Calmsden
Cirencester GL7 5ET
www.vanessaarbuthnott.co.uk
and
Country House Walks Ltd
Self-catering accommodation/
weekend breaks
The Tallet
Calmsden
Cirencester GL7 5ET
www.thetallet.co.uk
Pages 13br, 22, 31br, 137.

Piero Castellini Baldissera
Studio Castellini
via Morozzo della Rocco, 5
20123 Milan
Italy
studiocastellini@libero.it
Page 126r.

John Barman Inc.
Interior design and decoration
500 Park Avenue
New York NY 10022
USA
+1 212 838 9443
john@barman.com
www.johnbarman.com
Pages 33a, 120 all.

Belmont Freeman Architects
110 West 40 Street
New York, NY 10018
+1 212 382 3311
www.belmontfreeman.com
Page 69br.

Roberto Bergero
Interior designer
4 rue St. Gilles
75003 Paris
France
+33 1 42 72 03 51
robertobergero@club-internet.fr
Pages 16l, 39al.

Bruce Bierman Design, Inc.
Residential interior design firm
29 West 15th Street
New York NY 10011
USA
+1 212 243 1935
www.biermandesign.com
Page 117.

Stephen Blatt Architects
Architectural design firm
10 Danforth Street
Portland
Maine 04101
USA
+1 207 761 5911
sba@sbarchitects.com
Page 35ar.

L.B.D.A.
Laura Bohn Design Associates, Inc.
345 Seventh Avenue
2nd Floor
New York, NY 10001
USA
+1 212 645 3636
www.lbda.com
Pages 91ar, 127.

Ann Boyd Design Ltd
Studio 8
Fairbank Studios
Lots Road
London SW10 ONS
020 7351 4098
Page 7r.

Nancy Braithwaite Interiors
2300 Peachtree Road
Suite C101
Atlanta
Georgia 30309
USA
Page 3l.

Hugh Broughton Architects
Award-winning architects
4 Addison Bridge Place
London W14 8XP
020 7602 8840
www.hbarchitects.co.uk
Pages 1, 18l.

Buildburo
346 Fulham Road
London SW10 9UH
020 7352 1092
info@buildburo.co.uk
www.buildburo.co.uk
Page 131.

Cabot Design Ltd
Interior design
1925 Seventh Avenue, Suite 71
New York NY 10026
USA
+1 212 222 9488
eocabot@aol.com
Pages 3r, 6l, 14al, 17ar, 43c, 70br, 97al.

Milly de Cabrol Ltd
150 East 72nd Street, Suite 2-C
New York NY 10021
USA
+1 212 717 9317
Page 30b.

Marisa Tadiotto Cavalli
via Solferino, 11
20121 Milano
Italy
+39 03 48 41 01 738/
+39 02 86 46 24 26
+39 02 29 00 18 60
marisscavalli@hotmail.com
Page 31a.

Circus Architects
7 Brooks Court
Kirtling Street
London SW8 5BP
020 7627 6080
www.circus-architects.com
contact@circus-architects.com
Page 105b.

Collett Zarzycki Ltd
Fernhead Studios
2b Fernhead Road
London W9 3ET
020 8969 6967
mail@czltd.co.uk
Page 90.

The Color Wheel Company
www.colorwheelco.com
+1 541 929 7526
Page 19.

Conner Prairie Museum
134000 Alisonville Road
Fishers
Indiana 46038
USA
Page 43a.

Jo Crepain
Architect
Vlaandernstraat 6
8-2000 Antwerp
Belgium
+00 32 3 213 61 61
Page 84a.

Joëlle Darby
Architect
Darby Maclellan Partnership
Unit 3 Limehouse Cut
46 Morris Road
London E14 6NQ
020 7987 4432
darby.maclellan@tinyonline.co.uk
Page 112b.

Barbara Davis
Interior design; antique hand-dyed
linen, wool and silk textiles by the
yard; soft furnishings and clothes
to order.
USA
+1 607 264 36736
Pages 38br, 39ar, 39br, 81al.

Nanna Ditzel MDD FCSD
Industrial designer specializing in
furniture, textiles, jewellery and
exhibitions
Nanna Ditzel Design
Klareboderne 4
DK-1115 Copenhagen K
Denmark
www.nanna.ditzel.design.dk
Page 14ar.

Mary Drysdale
Drysdale, Inc.
78 Kalorama Cir NW
Washington DC 20008
+1 202 588 0700
Page 97ar.

Echo Design Agency
5 Sebastian Street
London EC1V 0HD
020 7251 6990
naomicleaver@echodesign.co.uk
Page 79b.

Emery & Cie and Noir D'Ivorie
Rue de l'Hôpital 25–29
Brussels
Belgium
+32 2 513 5892
Pages 77ar, 93a.

Jamie Falla
MOOArc
198 Blackstock Road
London N5 1EN
020 7345 1729
www.mooarc.com
Page 69ar.

Sarah Featherstone
Featherstone Associates
74 Clerkenwell Road
London EC1M 5QA
020 7490 1212
sarah.f@featherstone-
associates.co.uk
www.featherstone-associates.co.uk
Page 84b.

Gabellini Associates
665 Broadway
Suite 706
New York NY 10012
USA
+1 212 388 1700
www.gabelliniassociates.com
Page 71a.

Gloss Ltd
Designers of home accessories
274 Portobello Road
London W10 5TE
020 8960 4146
pascale@glossltd.u-net.com
Page 18r, 115b.

Yves Halard
Interior decoration
27 quai de la Tournelle
75005 Paris
France
+33 1 44 07 14 00
Pages 23l, 44 both, 91b, 119r, 128, 129c, 129b.

Alastair Hendy
Food writer, art director and
designer
fax 020 7739 6040
Pages 83al.

HM2 Architects
Architects and designers
Richard Webb, Project Director
Andrew Hanson, Director
33–37 Charterhouse Square
London EC1M 6EA
020 7600 5151
andrew.hanson@harper-
mackay.co.uk
Pages 28br, 100, 101, 121.

Anthony Hudson
Hudson Architects
49-59 Old Street
London EC1V 9HX
020 7490 3411
anthonyh@hudsonarchitects.co.uk
www.hudsonarchitects.co.uk
Norwich office t. 01603 755270
Page 84b.

Hut Sachs Studio
Architecture and interior design
414 Broadway
New York NY 10013
USA
+1 212 219 1567
hutsachs@hutsachs.com
www.hutsachs.com
Pages 109ar.

Janie Jackson
Stylist and designer
Parma Lilac
Children's nursery furnishings
and accessories
020 8960 9239
Page 48.

Jacksons
5 All Saints Road
London W11 1HA
020 7792 8336
Page 126l.

Daniel Jasiak
Designer
12 rue Jean Ferrandi
Paris 75006
France
+33 1 45 49 13 56
Pages 21ar, 86br, 87a.

Eva Johnson
Interior designer
Suffolk
01638 731362
www.evajohnson.co.uk
Page 61a.

KRD Kitchen Rogers Design
020 8944 7088
ab@krd.demon.co.uk
Page 99l.

Eric Liftin
Mesh Architecture
Architecture & web-site design &
development
180 Varick Street 11th floor
New York NY 10014
+1 212 989 3884
info@mesh-arc.com
www.mesh-arc.com
Page 29a.

Littman Goddard Hogarth
now Hogarth Architects
61 Courtfield Gardens
London SW5 0NQ
020 7565 8366
www.hogartharchitects.co.uk
info@hogartharchitects.co.uk
Pages 106a, 107.

Nicoletta Marazza
via G Morone, 8
20121 Milan
Italy
+39 2 7601 4482
Pages 92bl, 108b, 115a.

Marino + Giolito
161 West 16th Street
New York NY 10011
USA
+1 212 675 5737
Page 73a both.

Jean-Louis Ménard
32 boulevard de l'Hôpital
75005 Paris
France
+ 33 1 46 34 44 92
Page 61bl.

John Minshaw Designs Ltd
17 Upper Wimpole Street
London
W1H 6LU
020 7258 5777
enquiries@johnminshawdesigns.com
Page 74b.

Philippe Model
Decoration, home furnishing and
coverings
33 place du Marché St. Honoré
75001 Paris
France
+33 1 42 96 89 02
Page 14b.

The Moderns
900 Broadway, Suite 903
New York NY10003
USA
+1 212 387 8852
www.themoderns.com
moderns@aol.com
Page 62b.

Moneo Brock Studio
Francisco de Asis Mendez
Casariego 7 , Bajo
28002 Madrid
Spain
+34 91 563 8056
contact@moneobrock.com
www.moneobrock.com
Pages 94a, 109ar.

Lynn Morgan Design
118 Goodwives River Road
Darien, CT 06820
USA
+1 203 854 5037
Page 80b.

Elie Mouyal
rue Saâd Bnou Oubada n° 336 Issil
B. P.N° 3667 Amerchich
Marrakech
Morocco
+212 044 30 05 02/31 46 56
emouyal@iam.net.ma
*Pages 12al, 108a, 190ar, 109b,
109l, 111r both.*

Mimmi O'Connell
Shop: Port Of Call
Walton Street
London SW7
Page 12r.

Roger Oates Design
Shop and showroom:
1 Munro Terrace
off Cheyne Walk
London SW10 0DL
Studio Shop:
The Long Barn
Eastnor
Ledbury
Herefordshire HR8 1EL
Rugs and Runners mail-order
catalogue 01531 631611
www.rogeroates.co.uk
Page 60l.

Parnassus
corso Porta Vittoria, 5
Milan
Italy
+39 02 78 11 07
Page 38bl.

Plain English
Stowupland Hall
Stowupland
Stowmarket
Suffolk IP14 4BE
01449 774028
www.plainenglishdesign.com
Pages 57a, 92a.

Jennifer Post Design
Spatial and interior designer
25 East 67th Street, 8D
New York NY 10021
USA
+1 212 734 7994
jpostdesign@aol.com
Pages 67a, 78 both.

Géraldine Prieur
Interior designer
2, Boulevard Pershing
75017 Paris
France
+ 33 6 11 19 42 86
www.geraldineprieur.com
*Pages 6r, 24b, 36l, 45a,
122cl,122bl, 122r.*

Lena Proudlock
www.lenaproudlock.com
Pages 32r, 40a, 81b, 83bl, 87b.

Eric de Queker
DQ Design In Motion
Koninklijkelaan 44
2600 Bercham
Belgium
Pages 26, 61br, 71bl, 71bc.

Jonathan Reed
Studio Reed
151a Sydney Street
London SW3 6NT
020 7565 0066
Page 62ar.

Johanne Riss
Stylist, designer and fashion
designer
35 place du Nouveau Marché aux
Graens
1000 Brussels
Belgium
+32 2 513 09 00
www.johanneriss.com
Pages 51ar, 53al.

Charles Rutherfoord
51 The Chase
London SW4 0NP
020 7627 0182
www.charlesrutherfoord.net
Page 69l.

Josephine Ryan Antiques
63 Abbeville Road
London SW4 9JW
020 8675 3900
Page 53b.

Sophie Sarin
020 7221 4635
Page 125.

Sheila Scholes
Designer
01480 498241
Pages 41br, 58r.

Lloyd Schwan Design
195 Chrystie Street, # 908
New York NY 10002
USA
+1 212 375 0858
Page 32bl.

Sequana
64 avenue de la Motte Picquet
75015 Paris
France
+33 1 45 66 58 40
www.sequan.net
Pages 25ar, 96br.

Sharland & Lewis
45 Long Street
Tetbury
Gloucestershire GL8 8AA
01666 502440
www.sharlandandlewis.com
Page 13a.

Sheppard Day Design
020 7821 2002
Page 124.

Hunt Slonem
Artist
Represented by
Marlborough Gallery NYC
40 West 57th Street
New York NY 10019
USA
+1 212 541 4900
Page 30a.

Enrica Stabile
Antiques dealer, interior decorator
and photographic stylist
L'Utile e il Dilettevole
Via Carlo Maria Maggi 6
20154 Milano
+39 0234 53 60 86
www.enricastabile.com
Pages 86, 97b.

**John L. Stewart and Michael
D'Arcy of SIT**
SIT, L.L.C.
113–115 Bank Street
New York NY 10014-2176
USA
+1 212 620 777
JLSCollection@aol.com

Page 106b.
Stickland Coombe Architecture
258 Lavender Hill
London SW11 1LJ
020 7924 1699
www.sticklandcoombe.com
Pages 4–5, 23b, 35br, 68l, 79, 82.

Bruno Tanquerel
Artist
2 Passage St.Sébastien
75011 Paris
France
+33 1 43 57 03 93
Page 111l.

Touch Interior Design
020 7498 6409
Pages 41bl, 67b both, 68r both.

Urban Research Laboratory
3 Plantain Place
Crosby Row
London SE1 1YN
020 7403 2929
jeff@urbanresearchlab.com
*Pages 21b both, 33bl, 83ar, 85
all, 132b.*

Urban Salon Ltd
Architects
Unit D
Flat Iron Yard
Ayres Street
London SE1 1ES
020 7357 8000
www.urbansalonarchitects.com
Page 71br.

USE Architects
Unit 12
47–49 Tudor Road
London E9 7SN
020 8986 8111
www.usearchitects.com
Page 55al.

Hérve Vermesch
50 rue Bichat
75010 Paris
France
+33 1 42 01 39 39
Page 105al.

Miv Watts at House Bait
Interior decoration
Market Place
Burnham Market
Norfolk PE31 8HV
01358 730557
www.wattswishedfor.com
Pages 43b, 88b.

Voon Wong & Benson Saw
(formerly Voon Wong Architects)
Unit 3D Burbage House
83 Curtain Road
London EC2A 3BS
020 7033 8763
www.voon-benson.com
info@voon-benson.com
*Pages 27a both, 37b both, 94b,
160.*

José de Yturbe
De Yturbe Arquitectos
Patriotismo 13 (4o piso)
Lomas de Barrilaco
Mexico 11010 DF
Mexico
+00 525 540 368
deyturbeinfosel.net.mx
Page 28bl.

index

Page numbers in *italic* refer to captions and illustrations

A
accessories, as highlights 26–9
apricot *13*
aquamarine 94
Arts and Crafts *53, 58, 66, 67*, 110

B
bands, horizontal *27, 42*
bathrooms
black *71*
blue *83*
brown *65*
cream 61, *61*
fabrics *41*
gold *111*
green *15*, 89
greys *69*
mirrors *24*
orange *105*
white *55*
yellow 99, *99*
bedrooms
black *71*
blue *35, 81, 83, 84*
brown *64*
cream *60*
earth colours *17*
fabrics 41
gold 109
greens *14, 89*
lavender *126*
light *25*
lilac *123, 124*
neutral colours *7*
orange *43*
pink *123*
purple *130*
red *115, 119*
soft furnishings *39*
white *28, 53*
yellows 97, *97*
beiges 64–7
colour control 74–5
in combination 66–7
billiard rooms
black *17*
red 115
blackboard paint *29*, 71
blacks *17*, 70–3
all-black rooms 70
colour control 74–5

in combination 72–3
Blaue Reiter 17
blues 80–7
colour control 94–5
in combinations 84–7
brick 104
browns 64–7
colour control 74–5
in combination 66–7

C
calm colours 22–3
ceilings, dark colours 29
cerulean blue 83
children's rooms, yellow 99
Chinese blue 94
citrus yellow 99
cobalt 94
colour
choosing 34–7
defining space with 26–9
highlights 30–3
light and 22–5
perception of 16–17
properties 12–15
zoning with 26–9
colour blindness 16
colour boards 8, 34–6, *35, 76, 134*
colour control
bieges 74–5
blacks 74–5
blues 94–5
browns 74–5
creams 74–5
gold 112–13
greens 94–5
greys 74–5
lilac 132–3
neutrals 74-5
orange 112–13
pink 132–3
purple 132–3
red 132–3
silvers 74–5
whites 74–5
yellow 112–13
colour wheel 18–19, *19*
complementary colours 13, 18–19, 20–1
highlights 31
cool colours 17
highlights 33
coral 102, 104
cornelian 102

cottages
cream 59
greens 94
cotton fabrics 39–41
creams 58–63
all-cream schemes 58–61
colour control 74–5
in combination 62–3
crimson 115
curtains *30*

D
dado rails *6, 43*
dark rooms 24
dining and eating areas
blue *85, 87*
colours for 28
complementary colours *18*, 20
cream *58*
green *89*, 90, *90–1, 93*
purple *128–9*
soft furnishings *38*
white *54*
zoning 26
dirtied (knocked back) 13, *13, 18*

E
eating areas
blue *85, 87*
colours for 28
complementary colours *18*, 20
cream *58*
green *89*, 90, *90–1, 93*
purple *128–9*
soft furnishings *38*
white *54*
zoning 26
Eating Room Red 119
emerald 89, 93, 94
entrances, complementary colours 20
Etruscan Red 119

F
fabrics 38–41
beiges and browns 65
cream 60
white 53–4
Fauves 17
finishes, paint 42–5
floors 29
painted 44–5
white *52*, 53

Fox Red 119
furniture
blue 83
neutrals 75

G
gardens
influence of 93
inspiration from 130, 134
glass accessories *30*
gloss paint 42
gold leaf *45*
golds 108–11
colour control 112–13
in combination 110–11
grass green 91
greens 88–93
colour control 94–5
in combination 92–3
matching *6*
greys 68–9
colour control 74–5
in combination 72–3

H
halls
complementary colours 20
green 93
light sources 22
yellow 97
harmonious colours 18
heritage colours *14*
highlights 30–3
horizontal bands *27, 42*
hue, description 18

I
Impressionists 16–17
Indian red 102
indigo 81, 83, 84
inspirational sources 8, 36, 46, 76, 134
intensity, description 18

J
jade 91

K
kitchens
blue 81, *84, 86–7*
complementary colours 20, *20, 21*
cool colours *17*
cream 61
daring colours *18*
floors 29

gold *111*
green *29*, *91*, *92–3*
highlights *31*, *33*
lilac *125*
orange *105*
red *121*
white *54*, *54–5*
yellow 97, *98*
zoning 26–7
knocking back 13, *13*, 18

L
landings
 complementary colours 20
 light sources *24*
lavender 94
libraries, green 92
light
 effects of 15, *16*
 mirrors and *24*
 windows as source of
  23–5, *32*, *108*
lilacs 122–7
 colour control 132–3
 in combination 126
lime green *29*, 89, 94
lime yellow 99
linen, household 53
linen fabrics 39–41
living and sitting areas
 blacks 73
 browns *66–7*
 cream *59*
 gold *108*, *110*
 greens *88*, *91*
 greys *68*
 lilac *127*
 orange 6, *102–5*, *106–7*
 pinks *122*, *127*
 purple *130*
 red *115*, *116–17*, *118*,
  120
 white *7*, *50–1*
 yellows 6, *96–7*, 97,
  100–1
lofts, red 115

M
magenta 130
malachite 89, 93, 94
matt finishes 42
mauve 94
metallic finishes, wallpapers
 44
minimalism *55*, 65
mirrors and reds 121

monochrome *27*
mosaics, blue *83*

N
neutral colours 19, 47–74
 bedrooms *7*
 beiges 64–7
 blacks 70–3
 browns 64–7
 colour control 74–5
 creams 58–63
 greys 68–9
 inspiration for 46
 silvers 68–9
 whites 50–7
north-facing rooms 24
notebooks 8, 11, 134

O
off-white 43, 57, 62
olive greens 94
open-plan rooms, zoning
 26–9
optical tricks 12
oranges 102–7
 colour control 112–13
 in combination 106
oriental rooms *12*, *102–3*

P
paint
 choosing colours 34–7
 finishes 42–5
panelling, cream 59
pea green 91
period schemes, browns 67
photographs 8
pinks 122–7
 colour control 132–3
 in combination 126
plaster, unpainted *43*
primary colours 19
properties of colour 12–15
Prussian blue 81, 94
purples 129–31
 colour control 132–3
 in combination 130

R
racing green 89
ragging techniques *45*
raw sienna 104
recession 17
reds 114–21
 advancing *12*, *16*
 colour control 132–3

dining rooms *6*
 in combination 121
 oriental rooms *12*
rose pink 122
rural houses 59, 69
 lime green 94

S
sage green 94
saturation, description 18
Saxe blue 94
scarlet 115, 132
serenity 22–3
Seville orange 102
shades, description 19
shocking pink 122
shower rooms, blue *82*
silk fabrics 38–9, 41
silvers 68–9
 colour control 74–5
sitting and living areas
 blacks 73
 browns *66–7*
 cream *59*
 gold *108*, *110*
 greens *88*, *91*
 greys *68*
 lilac *127*
 orange 6, *102–5*, *106–7*
 pinks *122*, *127*
 purple *130*
 red *115*, *116–17*, *118*,
  120
 white *7*, *50–1*
 yellows 6, *96–7*, 97,
  100–1
soft colours *13*
soft furnishings 38–41
stairways
 red 117
 yellow 97
steel colours 68–9
stripes *14*, *28*, *41*, 44, *45*,
 97
 horizontal *27*, *42*
study areas
 highlights *32*
 orange *104*
Suffolk pink 103
sunlit rooms 24–5
swatches 8, 34–5, 75, 134

T
terracotta 102–6, 125
 dining rooms *6*
test pots 35, 75

textiles 38–41
 beiges and browns 65
 cream 60
 white 53–4
texture, colour and 38–41
throws *31*
tints, description 19
tone 13
 description 18, 19
turquoise 88, 89

U
ultramarine 81, 84

V
violet 130

W
wallpaper, metallic finishes
 44
warm colours *16*, 17
whites 40, 50–7
 accessories *40*
 all-white treatment *7*,
  50–5
 as a secondary colour *15*
 brilliant *41*
 colour control 74–5
 contrasting walls 28
 effects of light on 15
 in combination 56–7
 off-white 43, 57, 62
 with strong colours 57
windows, as light source
 23–5, *32*, *108*
wood
 browns 65
 floors 29, 44–5, *52*, 53
woollen fabrics 39
working areas
 highlights *32*
 orange *104*

Y
yellows *12*, 96–101
 colour control 112–13
 effects of light on 15
 in combination 100

Z
zoning space 26–9